Matrix Analysis of Interregional Population Growth and Distribution

MATRIX ANALYSIS
OF INTERREGIONAL
POPULATION GROWTH
AND DISTRIBUTION

BY ANDREI ROGERS

UNIVERSITY OF CALIFORNIA PRESS
BERKELEY AND LOS ANGELES/1968

University of California Press
Berkeley and Los Angeles, California

Cambridge University Press
London, England

Copyright © 1968, by
The Regents of the University of California

Library of Congress Catalog Card Number: 68-11530
Printed in the United States of America

To My Parents

PREFACE

My fundamental objective in writing this monograph has been to bring together, in a consistent and integrated manner, a body of theory that deals with an important aspect of mathematical demography: the analysis of interregional population growth and distribution by means of the algebra of matrices. The work reported here was initiated two years ago in a population and migration study conducted for the California State Development Plan. Subsequently, the research was supported by the Center for Planning and Development Research and, more recently, by the Institute of Social Sciences, both of the University of California at Berkeley.

In writing this essay, I am fully aware that a definitive work on population and space has not yet been written. Nor are texts on mathematical demography in plentiful supply. Nevertheless, this monograph does not seek to assume either of these roles. The scope of this study is narrow, focusing exclusively on a matrix approach to population analysis, and the topics that are discussed are those which are of particular interest to the author. As a result, readers expecting a comprehensive treatment of interregional population analysis may be disappointed. I have elected to write not a treatise, but an inquiry. The inquiry begins by introducing an interregional dimension to the demographer's well-known matrix model of population growth, and continues by examining whether such an extension leads to new insights and fertile directions for further study. It is hoped that this monograph may find use both as collateral reading in courses on mathematical demography and as a reference for professionals seeking a compact means for expressing and analyzing complex interregional demographic processes.

Many of the results summarized in this monograph originally appeared as papers in journals and conference proceedings. I am indebted to the various editors concerned for permission to reproduce substantial portions from the texts of those essays. Parts of Chapter 3 were originally published as "Sensitivity Tests of a Model of Population Growth in California Regions," *Papers of the Regional Science Association*, Western Section Proceedings, 1967. Portions of Chapters 2, 4, and 5 appeared in "Matrix Analysis of Interregional Population Growth and Distribution," *Papers of the Regional Science Association*, European Congress, XVIII, 1967. Some parts of Chapter 2 and Chapter 5 were originally included in "The Multiregional Matrix Growth Operator and the Stable Interregional Age Structure," *Demography*, III:2, 1966. Portions of Chapter 4 were published as "A Note on the Temporal Decomposition of Interpoint Transition Matrices," *Journal of Regional Science*, VI:2, 1966. Most of the material in Chapter 6 originally appeared as "A Markovian Policy Model of Interregional Migration," *Papers of the Regional Science Association*, National Meetings, XVII, 1966. Parts of Chapter 7 were drawn from "A Regression Analysis of Interregional Migration in California," *The Review of Economics and Statistics*, forthcoming, and from "A Markovian Analysis of Migration Differentials," *Proceedings of the Social Statistics Section of the American Statistical Association*, 126th Annual Meeting, 1966.

Finally, I wish to acknowledge the work of Nathan Keyfitz of the University of Chicago as the inspiration for the topics discussed in Chapters 2 and 5, and to thank LaVerne Marts for her masterful typing of the intricate matrix equations populating this monograph.

ANDREI ROGERS

Berkeley
April, 1967

CONTENTS

1. **Introduction** 1
   - Matrix Analysis 2
   - Estimation 3
   - Stability 3
   - Intervention 4
   - Migration 4
   - Conclusion 5

2. **The Fundamental Matrix Model of Interregional Population Growth and Distribution** 6
   - 2.1. Introduction 6
   - 2.2. The Interregional Components-of-Change Model . 6
   - 2.3. The Interregional Cohort-Survival Model . . . 10
   - 2.4. References 15

3. **Forecasting** 16
   - 3.1. Introduction 16
   - 3.2. A Simplified Interregional Cohort-Survival Model 16
   - 3.3. Fitting the Simplified Interregional Cohort-Survival Model to California Regions . . . 18
     - The Survivorship Matrix 19
     - The Migration Transition Matrices 19
     - Performance of the Simplified Interregional Cohort-Survival Model 22
   - 3.4. Forecasting with the Simplified Interregional Cohort-Survival Model 22
     - The Survivorship Matrix 22
     - The Migration Transition Matrices 24
     - Review of Findings 28
   - 3.5. References 30

4. Estimation 31
4.1. Introduction 31
4.2. Estimation by Temporal Decomposition . . . 31
4.3. Estimation on the Basis of Distributional Data . 35
    The Unrestricted Least-Squares Estimator . . . 38
    The Minimum Absolute Deviations Estimator . . 39
    The Restricted Least-Squares Estimator 42
4.4. References 43

5. Stability 46
5.1. Introduction 46
5.2. The Theory of Nonnegative Matrices and the Stable Interregional Population Distribution . . . 47
5.3. The Stable Interregional Population Distribution: California and the Rest of the United States . . . 49
    The Interregional Components-of-Change Model . 49
    The Interregional Cohort-Survival Model . . . 50
5.4. References 50

6. Intervention 53
6.1. Introduction 53
6.2. The Stationary Population System 54
    Intervention with Full Control 55
    The Kemeny-Snell Theorem 56
    Intervention with Partial Control 58
6.3. Interregional Distributional Goals and System Intervention in California: The Stationary Population Model 61
6.4. The Declining Population System 64
    Intervention with Full Control 66
    Intervention with Partial Control 67
6.5. The Expanding Population System 70
6.6. References 72

7. Migration 73
7.1. Introduction 73
7.2. Analysis of Migration Streams 73
    Migration Streams and Economic Opportunity . . 74
    Migration Streams by Class of Subregion at Origin and Destination 80

7.3. Analysis of Migration Differentials	82
Markovian Analysis of Migration Differentials	86
Migration Differentials in California: Some Empirical Results	92
7.4. Analysis of Differentiated Streams	104
7.5. References	110
8. Concluding Remarks	**112**
Index	**117**

TABLES

Table 2.1. Components of Population Change in California and the Rest of the United States: 1955–1960	8
Table 2.2. Migration Transition Matrix: 1955–60 (in 000's)	9
Table 3.1. Geographic Distribution of California's 1960 Population: Projected and Observed	24
Table 3.2. Migration Equation for Estimating the 25–29 Age Group Transition Proportions	26
Table 3.3. Geographic Distribution of California's Population: 1960 and 1980	27
Table 3.4. Age Composition of California's Population: 1960 and 1980	28
Table 3.5. Geographic Distribution of Net Migration in California: 1955–1960 and 1960–1980	29
Table 4.1. Interregional Distributions Generated by a Constant Growth Operator: California and the Rest of the United States: 1955–1960	34
Table 4.2. Interregional Migration Transition Matrix: 1955–1956 (in 000's)	35
Table 4.3. Components of Population Change in California and the Rest of the United States: 1955–1960	36
Table 4.4. Linear Programming Tableau for Finding the Minimum Absolute Deviations Estimate	40
Table 4.5. Linear Programming Tableau for the Two-Region Example	41

Table 4.6. Quadratic Programming Tableau for Finding the Restricted Least-Squares Estimate	43
Table 4.7. Quadratic Programming Tableau for the Two-Region Example	44
Table 5.1. Past and Asymptotic Interregional Population Distributions: California and the Rest of the United States	50
Table 5.2. Past and Asymptotic Interregional and Intraregional Age Structures: California and the Rest of the United States	51
Table 6.1. Three Region Example: No Intervention	61
Table 6.2. Three Region Example: Intervention with Full Control	61
Table 6.3. Three Region Example: Intervention with Partial Control	62
Table 6.4. Growth Operator, Stable Distribution, and the 1955 Population Distribution for California Regions and the Rest of the United States: The Stationary Population Model	62
Table 6.5. Stationary Population Model for California: Partial Control	65
Table 6.6. Alternative Distributional Goals for California Regions and Their Policy Implications: The Stationary Population Model with Partial Control	66
Table 6.7. Three Region Example: No Intervention	68
Table 6.8. Three Region Example: Intervention with Full Control	69
Table 6.9. Three Region Example: Intervention with Partial Control	69
Table 6.10. Three Region Example: Intervention with Full Control	71
Table 7.1. Regression Statistics for the Modified Lowry Model	77
Table 7.2. Regression Statistics for the Lowry-Rogers Model	79
Table 7.3. Regression Statistics for the Rogers Model	81
Table 7.4. Regression Statistics for Flows from Metropolitan Subregions	83

Table 7.5. Regression Statistics for Flows from Nonmetropolitan Subregions ... 84
Table 7.6. Transition Matrices and Equilibrium Distributions for California: By Time Period ... 94
Table 7.7. Transition Matrices and Equilibrium Distributions for California: By Color ... 95
Table 7.8. Transition Matrices and Equilibrium Distributions for California: By Age Group ... 96
Table 7.9. Transition Matrices and Equilibrium Distributions for California: By Age Group ... 97
Table 7.10. Transition Matrices and Equilibrium Distributions for California: By Age Group ... 98
Table 7.11. Transition Matrices and Equilibrium Distributions for California: By SMSA and Non-SMSA Flows ... 99
Table 7.12. Mean First Passage Times: By Time Period ... 100
Table 7.13. Mean First Passage Times: By Color ... 100
Table 7.14. Mean First Passage Times: By Age Group ... 101
Table 7.15. Interregional Distances ... 102
Table 7.16. Correlations Between Interregional Mean First Passage Times and Interregional Distances ... 102
Table 7.17. Regression Statistics for White and Non-White Flows ... 105
Table 7.18. Coefficients of Determination for the 17 Age-Specific Flow Matrices ... 106
Table 7.19. Regression Statistics for Selected Age Group Flows ... 107
Table 7.20. Regression Statistics for Selected Age Group Flows ... 108
Table 7.21. Regression Statistics for Male and Female Flows ... 109

FIGURES

Figure 2.1. The Multiregional Growth Process for California and the Rest of the United States: 1950–1960 ... 14
Figure 3.1. The Fertility Survivorship Matrix for California: 1955–1960 ... 20

Figure 3.2. 1955–1960 Age-Specific Migration Flows and Proportions Between 19 California Standard Economic Areas and the Rest of the United States: 30–34 Year Age Group   23

1 INTRODUCTION

Among available operational methods for analyzing and forecasting population growth and change, one may broadly distinguish between those models which are concerned only with total births, deaths, and migration from those which focus on the behavior of age and sex disaggregated cohorts. The former class of models typically are referred to as components-of-change models; the latter have been defined as cohort-survival models. Component models begin by analyzing the behavior of each of the major contributors to population change, that is, births, deaths, and migration and then combine this information with population data for a base period to establish an estimate of a future population. Cohort-survival models focus on the age distribution of a population on a given date and, by subjecting it to the appropriate age-specific rates of fertility, mortality, and mobility, arrive at the age distribution of survivors and descendants of the original population at successive intervals of time. In the interests of simplicity, the age-specific rates frequently are assumed to remain constant over the projection period, and often male and female cohorts are not identified for separate analysis.

Components-of-change models and cohort-survival models both manifest a dynamic but essentially aspatial structure. That is, they are recursive over time intervals, but typically operate on single-region populations. Spatial considerations are accommodated by replicating the analysis over as many areal units as comprise the study area. An interregional system, therefore, is analyzed one region at a time.

It is becoming increasingly evident that space and time are vital elements that need to be considered jointly in order to comprehend fully the inner workings of interregional systems. In economics, for example, the call by Isard for a redress of the imbalance created by a theoretical literature focusing almost exclusively on one-point economies has triggered concerted efforts toward the development of a general theory of location and space-economy.[1] Similarly, in demography the need for theories and methods which simultaneously consider the spatial as well as the temporal character of interrelated population processes is becoming a matter of increasing importance.

The fundamental objective of this study is to introduce the interregional dimension into the emerging theory of mathematical demography. The vehicle to be used for this extension is matrix algebra.

Matrix Analysis

Matrix algebra has been adopted by a generation of economists to express interindustry linkages and flows. In input-output models, for example, matrices are used to describe the interdependence of the activities of the many industries which constitute an economy. They could as easily be used to describe the interdependence of demographic processes across the many subareas comprising a region. In the first instance the division is sectoral, in the latter it is spatial.

Several recent research efforts in demography have taken advantage of the conceptual elegance and computational simplicity of matrix representation of population change and movement.[2] However, in every instance, the models describe a "closed" single region population that is subject only to the effects of births and deaths, and hence is undisturbed by migration. These models, therefore, are not directly applicable to studies of interregional systems of "open" subregions. Recent work in Markovian analysis of social and geographical mobility, however, suggests a natural extension of the demographer's single-region matrix model.[3]

---

[1] Walter Isard, *Location and Space-Economy* (New York: The Technology Press of Massachusetts Institute of Technology and John Wiley and Sons, 1956).

[2] Alvaro Lopez, *Problems in Stable Population Theory* (Princeton, N.J.: Office of Population Research, Princeton University, 1961); and Nathan Keyfitz, "The Population Projection as a Matrix Operator," *Demography*, I (1964), 56–73.

[3] Isadore Blumen, Marvin Kogan, and Philip J. McCarthy, *The*

Introduction

Perhaps the most important contribution of the matrix formulation of the population growth and distribution process is the separation of *process* from the *population* that is undergoing this process. The use of a projection operator to "grow" an interregional population system forward through time allows one to focus on the projection process itself, its application to another population, and its long-term implications. Moreover, the insights yielded by such an analysis are not attainable by conventional techniques of population analysis. Examples of this appear in problems of estimation, stability, intervention, and migration.

Estimation

Most efforts to analyze and forecast interregional population growth and distribution are constrained by the paucity of reliable data on interregional population movements. Migration data are simply not available for most regional subdivisions of the nation. As a result, demographers have turned to crude "residual" methods of estimating the migration component of change.[4] Recent efforts to express the interregional population growth process in matrix form, however, suggest a means for estimating a regime of growth solely on the basis of historical data on interregional population distributions.[5] This problem will be discussed in Chapter 4.

Stability

As with many models of economic phenomena, the conditions of birth and survivorship of a human population may be conveniently expressed in the form of a set of linear first-order homo-

---

Industrial Mobility of Labor as a Probability Process, Vol. VI, Cornell Studies of Industrial and Labor Relations (Ithaca, New York: The New York State School of Industrial and Labor Relations, Cornell University, 1955); and James D. Tarver and William R. Gurley, "A Stochastic Analysis of Geographical Mobility in Population Projections of the Census Divisions in the United States," *Demography*, II (1965), 134–139.

[4] J. S. Siegel and C. H. Hamilton, "Some Considerations in the Use of the Residual Method of Estimating Net Migration," *Journal of the American Statistical Association*, XLVII, 259 (September 1952), 475–500.

[5] Andrei Rogers and Robert Miller, "Estimating a Matrix Population Growth Operator from Distributional Time Series," *Annals of the Association of American Geographers*, forthcoming.

geneous difference equations with constant coefficients. In economics such models have triggered a literature on the stability implications of particular nonnegative matrices.[6] The same interest is beginning to be expressed by mathematical demographers. For example, it is now relatively well established that the dominant characteristic root of a survivorship matrix represents the intrinsic rate of growth of a population at stability, and the corresponding characteristic vector defines its asymptotic age distribution.[7] These results, however, have been derived only for single-region models. In Chapter 5, they are extended to interregional systems.

Intervention

Consider an interregional population system with n regions. During each unit interval of time a certain proportion of each region's population migrates to another region. At the same time, each region's population undergoes changes due to natural increase.

If left unchecked, the particular regime of growth that operates in such an interregional population system can produce highly undesirable results. For example, some regions may experience a dramatic decline in population, whereas others may end up with many more people than they can support. Hence intervention into the population system to effect a willful redistribution of population to regions may be desirable. This subject is examined in Chapter 6.

Migration

Current theories of internal migration view mobility as the resultant of the expulsive forces of adverse circumstances at a point of origin and the attractive powers of opportunities at a place of destination. Most commonly this point of view emphasizes the thesis that internal migration can best be explained as

---

[6] R. M. Solow, "On the Structure of Linear Models," *Econometrica*, XX (1952), 29–46; G. Debreu and I. N. Herstein, "Non-negative Square Matrices," *Econometrica*, XXI (1953), 597–607; M. A. Woodbury, "Characteristic Roots of Input-Output Matrices," in *Economic Activity Analysis*, O. Morgenstern (ed.), (New York: John Wiley and Sons, 1954), pp. 365–382.

[7] Lopez, *op. cit.*, pp. 36–40.

Introduction

a response to changing economic opportunities brought about by the differential impact of economic growth. Refinements of this thesis generally involve the disaggregation of migrant populations into cohorts which are homogeneous in their proclivity to migrate and in their response to socioeconomic variables. According to such theories, the probability that an individual moves from one region to another is a function of the characteristics of the individual and the characteristics of both the region of origin and the region of destination. These fundamental relationships are analyzed in Chapter 7.

Conclusion

Conceptualizing an interregional demographic process in matrix form confers advantages that are both notational and analytical in nature. Matrix notation often leads to insights that otherwise may have been obscured by more complicated expressions. For example, matrix representation of population growth and distribution leads to a convenient method for estimating the growth regime of a multiregional population system, in the absence of fertility, mortality, and mobility data. Moreover, formulating a problem in matrix terms also places at our disposal a large collection of theorems that have been proved about matrices. Thus available theorems concerning the stability properties of nonnegative matrices allow us to use the matrix model of interregional population change to deduce the ultimate growth and distributional consequences of current demographic trends and to gauge the scope and feasibility of policies aimed at redirecting the system away from the equilibrium that is indicated by such trends. In sum, as is so frequently true in theory building, what at first is introduced as a purely pragmatic and notationally elegant conceptualization ultimately becomes the vehicle for insights that are not obtainable by conventional methods of analysis.

2 THE FUNDAMENTAL MATRIX MODEL OF INTERREGIONAL POPULATION GROWTH AND DISTRIBUTION

2.1. Introduction

Current population forecasting efforts generally adopt variants of a projection technique which summarizes the pattern of fertility and mortality to which a population is subject and then explicitly introduces the effects of net migration. That is, an initial population is carried forward through a time period, say five years, by the appropriate application of birth and death rates and the allowance for changes due to net migration. Further degrees of refinement may be added by disaggregating the population into age, sex, and race differentiated cohorts which then are separately survived through time.

2.2. The Interregional Components-of-Change Model

The components method of population projection ordinarily is carried out by advancing an initial population forward through time by the repeated accounting of the effects of births, deaths, and net migration. Symbolically, the components-of-change model may be expressed as

(2.1) $$w^{(t+1)} = w^{(t)} + b^{(t)} - d^{(t)} + n^{(t)}$$

where $w^{(t)}$ = population at time t;
$b^{(t)}$ = number of births between t and $t+1$;
$d^{(t)}$ = number of deaths between t and $t+1$;
$n^{(t)}$ = number of net migrants between t and $t+1$.

Typically, b, d, and n are derived for each interval of time by the application of crude birth, death, and net migration rates so that

Fundamental Matrix Model

$$(2.2) \quad \begin{aligned} w^{(t+1)} &= w^{(t)} + \beta w^{(t)} - \delta w^{(t)} + \eta w^{(t)} \\ &= (1 + \beta - \delta + \eta)w^{(t)} = gw^{(t)} \end{aligned}$$

where β = crude birth rate;
  δ = crude death rate;
  η = crude net migration rate;
  g = the "growth multiplier."

As an illustration, consider the data in Table 2.1. Given the 1955 population for California, and the crude birth, death, and net migration rates that prevailed during the 1955–1960 period, we may apply (2.2) to estimate California's 1960 population (in thousands):

$$\begin{aligned} w^{(1960)} &= (1 + .1315 - .0473 + .0865)w^{(1955)} \\ &= (1.1707)12988 \\ &= 15205. \end{aligned}$$

In an analogous manner, we may derive the 1960 population for the rest of the United States which is presented in column 9 of Table 2.1.[1]

To apply the components-of-change model simultaneously to an interregional population system, we define the matrix counterpart of (2.2):

$$(2.3) \quad \mathbf{w}^{(t+1)} = (I + B - D + N)\mathbf{w}^{(t)} = G\mathbf{w}^{(t)}$$

where $\mathbf{w}^{(t)}$ = a column vector whose ith element denotes the population of region i at time t;
  I = an identity matrix;
  B, D, N = diagonal matrices whose nonzero elements denote the crude birth, death, and net migration rates of the m regions;
  $G = (I + B - D + N)$ = the matrix "growth operator."

Expressing the data in Table 2.1 in the form of (2.3), we have (in thousands):

$$\mathbf{w}^{(1960)} = \begin{bmatrix} 1.1707 & .0 \\ .0 & 1.0720 \end{bmatrix} \begin{bmatrix} 12988 \\ 152082 \end{bmatrix}$$

$$= \begin{bmatrix} 15205 \\ 163032 \end{bmatrix}.$$

---

[1] Discrepancies between tabular figures and those computed by the application of rates are due to rounding.

TABLE 2.1. COMPONENTS OF POPULATION CHANGE IN CALIFORNIA AND THE REST OF THE UNITED STATES: 1955–1960

(1) Region	(2) 1955 Population (000's)	(3) Births 1955–60 (000's)	(4) Deaths 1955–60 (000's)	(5) Net migration 1955–60 (000's)	(6) Crude birth rate	(7) Crude death rate	(8) Crude net migration rate	(9) 1960 Population (000's)
California	12,988	1,708	614	1,124	0.1315	0.0473	0.0865	15,206
Rest of the United States	152,082	19,499	7,417	−1,124	0.1282	0.0488	−0.0074	163,040
Total	165,070	21,207	8,031	—	—	—	—	178,246

SOURCE: U.S. Bureau of the Census, *Statistical Abstract of the United States: 1962* (Eighty-third edition), Washington, D.C., 1962, and California State Department of Finance, Financial and Population Research Section, *California Migration 1955–1960*, Sacramento, California, 1964. Without loss of generality, we assume that the total population of this two-region system is "closed," i.e., undisturbed by emigration and immigration. This assumption produces 1960 population totals that are slightly lower than those reported by the 1960 U.S. Census.

Fundamental Matrix Model

The above matrix formulation of the interregional components-of-change model allows us to introduce, without added effort, the separate effects of in- and out-migration. We begin by defining a migration transition matrix, P, whose elements, p_{ij}, describe the proportion of people who, during a specified time period, move from region i to region j. Such a transition matrix has been computed for our two-region system and appears in Table 2.2. We then replace, with its transpose, P', the matrices I and N in (2.3) to define the interregional population model

(2.4) $\quad \mathbf{w}^{(t+1)} = (B - D + P')\mathbf{w}^{(t)} = G\mathbf{w}^{(t)}$

where $G = (B - D + P') =$ the matrix "growth operator."

TABLE 2.2. MIGRATION TRANSITION MATRIX: 1955–60 (in 000's)

From \ To	California	U.S.	1955 Total population
California	12,174 (.9373)	814 (.0627)	12,988 (1.0000)
Rest of the United States	1,938 (.0127)	150,144 (.9873)	152,082 (1.0000)

SOURCE: California State Department of Finance, Financial and Population Research Section, *California Migration 1955–1960*, Sacramento, California, 1964.

Expressing the data in Tables 2.1 and 2.2 in the form of (2.4), we once again may solve for the 1960 populations in our two-region system:

(2.5) $\quad \mathbf{w}^{(1960)} = \begin{bmatrix} 1.0215 & .0127 \\ .0627 & 1.0667 \end{bmatrix} \begin{bmatrix} 12988 \\ 152082 \end{bmatrix}$
$= \begin{bmatrix} 15199 \\ 163040 \end{bmatrix}.$

The components-of-change model confounds mortality, fertility, and mobility with age. For a more realistic application of birth, death, and migration rates, demographers have turned to the definition of more homogeneous population groups for projection purposes. A step in this direction is the disaggregation of a total population into separate age groups, or "cohorts," and the application of age-specific rates to these groups over time. This extension of the simple components-of-change model is commonly referred to as the cohort-survival model.

2.3. The Interregional Cohort-Survival Model

Mathematical demographers have demonstrated that the process of surviving an age distribution forward through time may be expressed by means of matrix multiplication.[2] Their fundamental model may be summarized by the equation:

(2.6) $$\mathbf{w}^{(t+1)} = S\mathbf{w}^{(t)},$$

where

$$S_{n \times n} = \begin{bmatrix} 0 & 0 \ldots b_1 & b_2 \ldots b_u & 0 \ldots 0 \\ {}_1d_2 & 0 & 0 & \ldots & 0 \\ 0 & {}_2d_3 & 0 & \ldots & 0 \\ 0 & 0 & {}_3d_4 & \ldots & 0 \\ \vdots & & & \ddots & \vdots \\ 0 & 0 & 0 & \ldots {}_{n-1}d_n & 0 \end{bmatrix} \quad \mathbf{w}^{(t)} = \begin{bmatrix} w_1^{(t)} \\ w_2^{(t)} \\ \vdots \\ \\ \\ w_n^{(t)} \end{bmatrix}$$

and $w_r^{(t)}$ = the population in the rth age group at time t;
$\quad b_r$ = the number of births that "survive" to the end of the unit time interval, per person, in the rth child-bearing age group;
$\quad {}_rd_{r+1}$ = the proportion of people in the rth age group who survive to the $r + 1$st age group after the unit time interval.

The contribution of net migration to population change in the above system, during the interval $(t, t + 1)$, may be denoted by the vector $\mathbf{n}^{(t)}$. Thus

(2.7) $$\mathbf{w}^{(t+1)} = S\mathbf{w}^{(t)} + \mathbf{n}^{(t)}.$$

For a matrix, M, which when applied to $\mathbf{w}^{(t)}$ will generate the net migration vector $\mathbf{n}^{(t)}$, we define a matrix operator which satisfies the following equation:

(2.8) $$\mathbf{n}^{(t)} = M\mathbf{w}^{(t)}.$$

---

[2] See, for example: Nathan Keyfitz, "Matrix Multiplication as a Technique of Population Analysis," *Milbank Memorial Fund Quarterly*, XLII, 4 (October 1964), 68–83; and Alvaro Lopez, *Problems in Stable Population Theory* (Princeton, N.J.: Office of Population Research, 1961).

Fundamental Matrix Model

Such an operator is:

$$\underset{n \times n}{M} = \begin{bmatrix} 0 & 0 & 0 & \ldots & 0 \\ m_1 & 0 & 0 & \ldots & 0 \\ 0 & m_2 & 0 & \ldots & 0 \\ 0 & 0 & m_3 & \ldots & 0 \\ \cdot & \cdot & & & \cdot \\ \cdot & \cdot & & \cdot & \cdot \\ 0 & 0 & 0 & \ldots m_{n-1} & 0 \end{bmatrix}$$

where $m_i = $ the net migration rate for the ith age group.

Now the effects of survivorship and migration may be combined simply by adding the matrices S and M to define a "growth" matrix, G. This transforms (2.7) into:

(2.9) $$\mathbf{w}^{(t+1)} = G\mathbf{w}^{(t)}.$$

The demographer's single-region matrix cohort-survival model as expressed by (2.6) for "closed" populations and by (2.9) for "open" populations may be extended to include interregional systems. We begin by attaching a subscript to each population vector, $\mathbf{w}$, and to every survivorship matrix, S, i.e.,

(2.10) $$\mathbf{w}_i^{*(t+1)} = S_i \mathbf{w}_i^{(t)} \qquad (i = 1, \ldots, m).$$

At this point an asterisk reminds us that a component of change unique to interregional population systems, i.e., migration, still needs to be incorporated. Since the effects of out-migration may be included in the survivorship proportions, $_r d_{r+1}$, only the contribution of in-migration still needs to be expressed. Finally, it should be noted that, in order to maintain the convenience of a single matrix operator, we may adopt the algebra of partitioned matrices and apply (2.10) to all m regions in one step:

(2.11) $$\begin{bmatrix} \mathbf{w}_1^{*(t+1)} \\ \mathbf{w}_2^{*(t+1)} \\ \cdot \\ \cdot \\ \cdot \\ \mathbf{w}_m^{*(t+1)} \end{bmatrix} = \begin{bmatrix} S_1 & 0 & 0 & \ldots & 0 \\ 0 & S_2 & 0 & & \vdots \\ 0 & 0 & S_3 & & \vdots \\ \vdots & & & \ddots & 0 \\ 0 & \ldots & \ldots & 0 & S_m \end{bmatrix} \begin{bmatrix} \mathbf{w}_1^{(t)} \\ \mathbf{w}_2^{(t)} \\ \cdot \\ \cdot \\ \cdot \\ \mathbf{w}_m^{(t)} \end{bmatrix}.$$

Consider migration as a component of population change in an interregional system. Associated with every region, i, is a population vector, $\mathbf{w}_i$. During each unit interval of time, a certain fraction of the ith region's population, in a given age group, r, migrates to region j and enters the $r + $ 1st age group there. Thus for each age group we may construct an interregional transition matrix, $_rP_{r+1}$, which describes the proportion of people, in the rth age group in region i, who during the specified time period move into the $r + $ 1st age group in region j:

$$(2.12) \quad \begin{matrix} _rP_{r+1} \\ m \times m \end{matrix} = \begin{bmatrix} _{r,1}p_{r+1,1} & _{r,1}p_{r+1,2} & \cdots & _{r,1}p_{r+1,m} \\ _{r,2}p_{r+1,1} & _{r,2}p_{r+1,2} & \cdots & \cdot \\ \cdot & & \cdot & \cdot \\ \cdot & & \cdot & \cdot \\ \cdot & & & \cdot \\ _{r,m}p_{r+1,1} & \cdots\cdots\cdots & _{r,m}p_{r+1,m} \end{bmatrix}$$

$(r = 1, \ldots, n).$

With an estimated set of n transition matrices, we may construct a series of matrix operators, M_{ij}, which when applied to the age distribution at i will "migrate" the requisite number of people from region i to region j and survive them into the next age cohort:

$$(2.13) \quad \mathbf{k}_{ij} = M_{ij}\mathbf{w}_i^{(t)},$$

where

$$\begin{matrix} M_{ij} \\ n \times n \end{matrix} = \begin{bmatrix} 0 & 0 & \cdots\cdots\cdots & 0 \\ _{1,i}p_{2,j} & 0 & \cdots\cdots\cdots & 0 \\ 0 & _{2,i}p_{3,j} & 0 & \\ \cdot & & \cdot & \cdot \\ \cdot & & & \cdot \\ \cdot & & & \cdot \\ 0 & \cdots\cdots\cdots & _{n-1,i}p_{n,j} & 0 \end{bmatrix} \quad \mathbf{k}_{ij} = \begin{bmatrix} 0 \\ _2k_{ij} \\ \cdot \\ \cdot \\ \cdot \\ \cdot \\ _nk_{ij} \end{bmatrix}$$

and

$_rk_{ij} = $ the total number of in-migrants, in the rth age group, into region j from region i.

Summing the in-migrants over all origins, i, we find the total in-migration into region j:

$$(2.14) \quad _rk_{\cdot j} = \sum_i {}_rk_{ij} \quad (r = 1, 2, \ldots, n).$$

Fundamental Matrix Model

As in the case of the fertility-mortality process, we may introduce partitioned matrices to express (2.14). For example, for $i = 1$:

(2.15)
$$\mathbf{k}_{.1} = \begin{bmatrix} 0 & | & M_{21} & | & M_{31} & | & \ldots & | & M_{m1} \end{bmatrix} \begin{bmatrix} \mathbf{w}_1^{(t)} \\ \mathbf{w}_2^{(t)} \\ \vdots \\ \mathbf{w}_m^{(t)} \end{bmatrix}.$$

Thus for $j = 1, 2, \ldots, m$ we have:

(2.16)
$$\begin{bmatrix} \mathbf{k}_{.1} \\ \mathbf{k}_{.2} \\ \cdot \\ \cdot \\ \cdot \\ \mathbf{k}_{.m} \end{bmatrix} = \begin{bmatrix} 0 & | & M_{21} & | & M_{31} & | & \ldots & | & M_{m1} \\ M_{12} & | & 0 & | & M_{32} & | & \ldots & | & M_{m2} \\ M_{13} & | & M_{23} & | & 0 & | & \ldots & | & M_{m3} \\ \cdot & & \cdot & & & & & & \cdot \\ \cdot & & \cdot & & & & & & \cdot \\ M_{1m} & | & \ldots & | & \ldots & | & \ldots & | & 0 \end{bmatrix} \begin{bmatrix} \mathbf{w}_1^{(t)} \\ \mathbf{w}_2^{(t)} \\ \cdot \\ \cdot \\ \cdot \\ \mathbf{w}_m^{(t)} \end{bmatrix}$$

The combined effects of fertility, mortality, and geographical mobility on an interregional population system may be expressed by adding the "super" matrix operators in (2.11) and (2.16). This defines an overall "growth" matrix operator, G, which when applied to an interregional population distribution will carry it forward through time. That is:

$$G = \begin{bmatrix} S_1 & | & M_{21} & | & M_{31} & | & \ldots & | & M_{m1} \\ M_{12} & | & S_2 & | & M_{32} & | & \ldots & | & M_{m2} \\ M_{13} & | & M_{23} & | & S_3 & | & \ldots & | & M_{m3} \\ \cdot & & & & \cdot & & & & \cdot \\ \cdot & & & & \cdot & & & & \cdot \\ M_{1m} & | & \ldots & | & \ldots & | & \ldots & | & S_m \end{bmatrix} \quad \mathbf{w}^{(t)} = \begin{bmatrix} \mathbf{w}_1^{(t)} \\ \mathbf{w}_2^{(t)} \\ \cdot \\ \cdot \\ \cdot \\ \mathbf{w}_m^{(t)} \end{bmatrix}$$

and

(2.17) $$\mathbf{w}^{(t+1)} = G\mathbf{w}^{(t)}.$$

Each submatrix, S_i, in G, now accounts for the effects of fertility and mortality in region i and for the migration out of region i.[3]

---

[3] The $_r d_{r+1}$ of the matrices, S_i, need to be modified so as to include

$$
\underset{1960}{\underline{w} = \begin{pmatrix} w_{Cal} \\ w_{US} \end{pmatrix}} \qquad G = \begin{pmatrix} \frac{S_{Cal}}{M_{Cal,US}} & \frac{M_{US,Cal}}{S_{US}} \end{pmatrix} \qquad \underset{1950}{\underline{w} = \begin{pmatrix} w_{Cal} \\ w_{US} \end{pmatrix}}
$$

$$
\left[\begin{array}{c}
3346 \\ 2514 \\ 2000 \\ 2319 \\ 2045 \\ 1528 \\ 1102 \\ 655 \\ 208 \\ \hline
35667 \\ 27478 \\ 19670 \\ 22111 \\ 20434 \\ 16508 \\ 12298 \\ 7393 \\ 2046
\end{array}\right]
=
\left[\begin{array}{ccccccccc|ccccccccc}
0 & .3375 & 1.1861 & .4789 & .0424 & 0 & 0 & 0 & 0 & 0 & 0 & 0 & 0 & 0 & 0 & 0 & 0 & 0 \\
.8731 & 0 & 0 & 0 & 0 & 0 & 0 & 0 & 0 & .0297 & 0 & 0 & 0 & 0 & 0 & 0 & 0 & 0 \\
0 & .9228 & 0 & 0 & 0 & 0 & 0 & 0 & 0 & 0 & .0399 & 0 & 0 & 0 & 0 & 0 & 0 & 0 \\
0 & 0 & .7821 & 0 & 0 & 0 & 0 & 0 & 0 & 0 & 0 & .0450 & 0 & 0 & 0 & 0 & 0 & 0 \\
0 & 0 & 0 & .7891 & 0 & 0 & 0 & 0 & 0 & 0 & 0 & 0 & .0316 & 0 & 0 & 0 & 0 & 0 \\
0 & 0 & 0 & 0 & .6905 & 0 & 0 & 0 & 0 & 0 & 0 & 0 & 0 & .0300 & 0 & 0 & 0 & 0 \\
0 & 0 & 0 & 0 & 0 & .7938 & 0 & 0 & 0 & 0 & 0 & 0 & 0 & 0 & .0145 & 0 & 0 & 0 \\
0 & 0 & 0 & 0 & 0 & 0 & .6288 & 0 & 0 & 0 & 0 & 0 & 0 & 0 & 0 & .0137 & 0 & 0 \\
0 & 0 & 0 & 0 & 0 & 0 & 0 & .3540 & 0 & 0 & 0 & 0 & 0 & 0 & 0 & 0 & .0126 & 0 \\ \hline
0 & 0 & 0 & 0 & 0 & 0 & 0 & 0 & 0 & 0 & .2257 & .9746 & .4252 & .0364 & 0 & 0 & 0 & 0 \\
.1682 & 0 & 0 & 0 & 0 & 0 & 0 & 0 & 0 & .9903 & 0 & 0 & 0 & 0 & 0 & 0 & 0 & 0 \\
0 & .1503 & 0 & 0 & 0 & 0 & 0 & 0 & 0 & 0 & .9523 & 0 & 0 & 0 & 0 & 0 & 0 & 0 \\
0 & 0 & .2536 & 0 & 0 & 0 & 0 & 0 & 0 & 0 & 0 & .9843 & 0 & 0 & 0 & 0 & 0 & 0 \\
0 & 0 & 0 & .1565 & 0 & 0 & 0 & 0 & 0 & 0 & 0 & 0 & .9594 & 0 & 0 & 0 & 0 & 0 \\
0 & 0 & 0 & 0 & .0988 & 0 & 0 & 0 & 0 & 0 & 0 & 0 & 0 & .9176 & 0 & 0 & 0 & 0 \\
0 & 0 & 0 & 0 & 0 & .0670 & 0 & 0 & 0 & 0 & 0 & 0 & 0 & 0 & .8499 & 0 & 0 & 0 \\
0 & 0 & 0 & 0 & 0 & 0 & .0583 & 0 & 0 & 0 & 0 & 0 & 0 & 0 & 0 & .7171 & 0 & 0 \\
0 & 0 & 0 & 0 & 0 & 0 & 0 & .0560 & 0 & 0 & 0 & 0 & 0 & 0 & 0 & 0 & .3921 & 0
\end{array}\right]
\left[\begin{array}{c}
1947 \\ 1283 \\ 1698 \\ 1750 \\ 1438 \\ 1125 \\ 819 \\ 404 \\ 122 \\ \hline
27417 \\ 20453 \\ 22026 \\ 21013 \\ 17836 \\ 14382 \\ 10243 \\ 5160 \\ 1581
\end{array}\right]
$$

Fig. 2.1. The multiregional growth process for California and the rest of the United States, 1950–1960. Population data in thousands.

The matrices M_{ij} account for the migration of people into region j from all origins $i(i \neq j)$.

For an illustration of the multiregional growth process, consider the matrix operation presented in Figure 2.1.[4] There, a vector denoting the 1950 population for our two-region system consisting of California and the rest of the United States, by ten-year age groups, is projected forward through time by a ten-year growth operator. The matrix multiplication introduces the combined effects of interregional mortality, fertility, and mobility and establishes their joint contribution to the interregional growth process.

2.4. References

[1] Keyfitz, Nathan, "Matrix Multiplication as a Technique of Population Analysis," *Milbank Memorial Fund Quarterly*, XLII, 4 (October 1964), 68–83.

[2] ———, "The Population Projection as a Matrix Operator," *Demography*, I (1964), 56–73.

[3] Leslie, P. H., "On the Use of Matrices in Certain Population Mathematics," *Biometrika*, XXXIII (November 1945), 183–212.

[4] ———, "Some Further Notes on the Use of Matrices in Population Mathematics," *Biometrika*, XXXV (December 1948), 213–245.

[5] Lopez, Alvaro, *Problems in Stable Population Theory* (Princeton, N.J.: Office of Population Research, 1961).

[6] Rogers, Andrei, "Matrix Methods of Population Analysis," *Journal of the American Institute of Planners*, XXXII, 1 (January 1966), 40–44.

[7] ———, "The Multiregional Matrix Growth Operator and the Stable Interregional Age Structure," *Demography*, III, 2 (1966), 537–544.

---

the effects of out-migration. That is, they now denote the proportion of people in the rth age group in region i who, after a unit time interval, are survived into the $r + $ 1st age group *in the same region*.

[4] Because migration data for the 1950–1960 interval were not available, the elements of the matrix operator were estimated so as to exactly reproduce the 1960 population vector. Thus California's 1960 population in Figure 2.1 differs slightly from that derived in Table 2.1.

3 FORECASTING

3.1. Introduction

Experience with matrix models in population forecasting is relatively limited. However, recent efforts already have demonstrated the utility of the matrix formulation. The interregional cohort-survival model outlined in Chapter 2, with a few simplifying assumptions to accommodate a substantial increase in the number of regions, has been used to forecast California's interregional population, by five-year cohorts, to 1980.[1] The model was fitted using 1955–1960 data on the state's 19 State Economic Areas; migration was forecast at each iteration by an "economic opportunities" regression model, and alternate sets of population projections were generated on the basis of various mixes of assumptions regarding fertility patterns and general economic growth. The model and some of the results it generated are summarized in this chapter.

3.2. A Simplified Interregional Cohort-Survival Model

The interregional cohort-survival model outlined in Chapter 2 requires extensive fitting and a great many arithmetical operations when applied to interregional systems composed of many regions. On such occasions it is often desirable to find a more economic solution by reducing the number of parameters to be fitted and multiplications to be performed. Simplification of the model, of course, incurs a cost in terms of its accuracy; however, the importance of accuracy must be weighed against the costs of precision.

Recall the interregional cohort-survival model defined by

---

[1] Andrei Rogers, *Projected Population Growth in California Regions: 1960–1980*, Center for Planning and Development Research, University of California, Berkeley, December 1965.

Forecasting

(2.17), and consider the simplification that is achieved by assuming age-specific birth and death rates to be the same for all regions in the system. This results in the following reduction of (2.11):

$$
(3.1)\quad
\begin{bmatrix} \mathbf{w}_1^{*(t+1)} \\ \mathbf{w}_2^{*(t+1)} \\ \vdots \\ \mathbf{w}_m^{*(t+1)} \end{bmatrix}
=
\begin{bmatrix}
S & 0 & 0 & \cdots & 0 \\
0 & S & 0 & & \vdots \\
0 & 0 & S & \cdot & \vdots \\
\vdots & & \cdot & \cdot & 0 \\
0 & \cdots & \cdots & 0 & S
\end{bmatrix}
\begin{bmatrix} \mathbf{w}_1^{(t)} \\ \mathbf{w}_2^{(t)} \\ \vdots \\ \mathbf{w}_m^{(t)} \end{bmatrix}
$$

$$= S[\mathbf{w}_1^{(t)}, \mathbf{w}_2^{(t)}, \ldots, \mathbf{w}_m^{(t)}] = SW.$$

Now recall the interregional migration transition matrices, defined by (2.12), which describe the number of people, in the rth age group in region i, who during the specified time period move into the $r + 1$st age group in region j:

$$
(3.2)\quad
{}_rP_{r+1} \atop m \times m
=
\begin{bmatrix}
{}_{r,1}p_{r+1,1} & {}_{r,1}p_{r+1,2} & \cdots & {}_{r,1}p_{r+1,m} \\
{}_{r,2}p_{r+1,1} & {}_{r,2}p_{r+1,2} & \cdots & \cdot \\
\cdot & \cdot & & \cdot \\
\cdot & \cdot & & \cdot \\
\cdot & \cdot & & \cdot \\
{}_{r,m}p_{r+1,1} & \cdots & \cdots & {}_{r,m}p_{r+1,m}
\end{bmatrix}
\quad (r = 1, \ldots, n).
$$

With a particular ${}_rP_{r+1}$ and the interregional distribution of the population in the rth age group, $\mathbf{w}'_r$ (i.e., the rth row vector in the population matrix W), we may obtain the corresponding interregional age-specific flow matrix, say ${}_rK_{r+1}$. We merely apply the transition matrix ${}_rP_{r+1}$ to a diagonal matrix, A_r, whose non-zero elements denote each region's population in the rth age group. That is, for each age group:

$$(3.3)\qquad A_{rr}P_{r+1} = {}_rK_{r+1} \qquad (r = 1, 2, \ldots, n).$$

Given the total number of people in each age group who move from region i to region j and into the next age group, after an interval of time $(t, t+1)$, we can find the age-distributed net migration component for each of the m regions by subtracting the total number of out-migrants from the total number of in-migrants. In matrix notation:

$$\mathbf{n}'_{i,t} = \mathbf{1}'K_i - (K_i\mathbf{1})'$$

and

(3.4) $$N_t = \begin{bmatrix} \mathbf{n}'_{1,t} \\ \mathbf{n}'_{2,t} \\ \cdot \\ \cdot \\ \cdot \\ \mathbf{n}'_{n,t} \end{bmatrix}.$$

With these revised methods for handling each of the major components of population change, we now have the following simplified version of (2.17):

(3.5) $$W_{t+1} = SW_t + N_t,$$

where W_t = a population matrix whose rows denote age groups and whose columns denote regions;

S = a fertility-survivorship matrix which is constant over the m regions of the system;

N_t = a net migration matrix whose rows denote age groups and whose columns denote regions.

3.3. Fitting the Simplified Interregional Cohort-Survival Model to California Regions

Changes in the size and distribution of the population in any region arise from the interrelationships between three components of change: births, deaths, and net migration. In California, considerable differences have emerged in the rates of growth of the various subregions of the state. These differences have strikingly affected both the distribution and the composition of its population.

A focus on the details of population growth in each of the state's 58 counties would obscure the more significant differences in interregional relationships. Moreover, the volume of detail that would be necessary for a sophisticated analysis would tax even the latest generation of computers. On the other hand, a treatment of the state as a whole would conceal major features of interregional population growth and movement. Therefore, it is desirable to adopt a system of regions which is satisfactory both from the standpoint of providing relatively homogeneous social and economic populations and which, in addition, has been a fundamental statistical framework for the collection and tabulation of data collected by state and federal agencies. These

Forecasting

considerations suggest the use of the state's 10 metropolitan and 9 nonmetropolitan State Economic Areas in 1960,[2] and, to close the system, the region consisting of the rest of the United States.[3] Hence the simplified interregional cohort-survival model was fitted to a 20 region system.

The Survivorship Matrix

The survivorship matrix used for testing the growth model appears in Figure 3.1. The elements of the top row may be interpreted as the number of births that survive to the end of the five-year interval, per person, in the rth child-bearing age group. (The "child-bearing" age groups were assumed to begin with the 15–19 age group and end with the 40–44 age group.) The subdiagonal survival elements denote the proportion of people, from a given age group, who survive to the following age group during a five-year period. Both sets of proportions were estimated using unpublished data from the California State Department of Public Health.[4]

The Migration Transition Matrices[5]

The matrix model defined by (3.5) requires, as inputs, age-specific transition matrices which describe the proportion of

---

[2] California had 10 SMSA's in 1960. Since then, two additional SMSA's have been created: the Vallejo-Napa SMSA and the Anaheim-Santa Ana-Garden Grove SMSA. In addition, the counties of Yolo and Placer have been added to the Sacramento SMSA. However, because of the absence of historical data on these areal units (e.g., migration flows), the changes were not incorporated in the analyses reported here.

[3] For convenience, we assume that the United States is undisturbed by emigration and immigration.

[4] The population of "the rest of the United States" was carried along as a twentieth region. However, California birth and death rates were not applied to the twentieth region. Rather, it was assumed that the United States population will follow the U.S. Bureau of the Census Series B projections. (U.S. Bureau of the Census, *Projections of the Population of the United States, By Age and Sex: 1964 to 1985*, Series P-25, No. 286, July 1964.) At the beginning of each five-year iteration, the California projection was subtracted from the U.S. Census Series B total to derive the population of the twentieth region.

[5] The number of net migrants in the 0–4 age group, at each iteration, cannot be derived by the application of five-year transition matrices. Therefore, this figure was assumed to be a function of the total number

$$S = \begin{bmatrix}
0 & .2884 & .7762 & .4969 & .2762 & .1380 & .0321 & 0 & 0 & 0 & 0 & 0 & 0 & 0 & 0 & 0 & 0 \\
.9964 & 0 & 0 & 0 & 0 & 0 & 0 & 0 & 0 & 0 & 0 & 0 & 0 & 0 & 0 & 0 & .3942 \\
0 & .9977 & 0 & 0 & 0 & 0 & 0 & 0 & 0 & 0 & 0 & 0 & 0 & 0 & 0 & .6274 & 0 \\
0 & 0 & .9979 & 0 & 0 & 0 & 0 & 0 & 0 & 0 & 0 & 0 & 0 & 0 & .7585 & 0 & 0 \\
0 & 0 & 0 & .9949 & 0 & 0 & 0 & 0 & 0 & 0 & 0 & 0 & 0 & .8427 & 0 & 0 & 0 \\
0 & 0 & 0 & 0 & .9929 & 0 & 0 & 0 & 0 & 0 & 0 & 0 & .8924 & 0 & 0 & 0 & 0 \\
0 & 0 & 0 & 0 & 0 & .9932 & 0 & 0 & 0 & 0 & 0 & .9288 & 0 & 0 & 0 & 0 & 0 \\
0 & 0 & 0 & 0 & 0 & 0 & .9922 & 0 & 0 & 0 & .9507 & 0 & 0 & 0 & 0 & 0 & 0 \\
0 & 0 & 0 & 0 & 0 & 0 & 0 & .9876 & 0 & .9686 & 0 & 0 & 0 & 0 & 0 & 0 & 0 \\
0 & 0 & 0 & 0 & 0 & 0 & 0 & 0 & .9814 & 0 & 0 & 0 & 0 & 0 & 0 & 0 & 0 \\
\end{bmatrix}$$

Fig. 3.1. The fertility survivorship matrix for California, 1955–1960.

people in the *r*th age group who, during a five-year period, move from region *i* to region *j* and into the next age group. Such detailed information was not available and, therefore, had to be estimated from U.S. Census data.

The 1960 Census of Population (Series PC (2-2B)) reports the 1955 State Economic Area residence of all persons 5 years and older in 1960. These data provide the necessary information for the construction of a place-to-place flow table. Component detail (age, color, sex, and so on) is not given for inter-SEA flows; however, this information is available for both total in- and out-flows. Thus it is possible, with the use of a few simple assumptions, to decompose the reported 1955–1960 total inter-SEA flow matrix into 17 age-specific flow matrices by the following steps:

(1) Assume that the age distribution of the total number of out-migrants from each SEA to every other SEA was the same for all destinations. That is, assume the age composition of each flow from *i* to *j* was the same for all $j (j \neq i)$ and, in particular, was equal to the age distribution of all out-migrants from *i*. On the basis of this assumption, decompose the total flow matrix into 17 age-specific flow matrices.

(2) Repeat the above procedure using the assumption that the age distribution of the total number of in-migrants to each SEA from every other SEA was the same from all origins.

(3) Average the two sets of matrices to obtain an estimate of the 17 age-specific inter-SEA and interstate flows for the 1955–1960 period.

(4) Finally, estimate the 1955 age distribution for each SEA by interpolating between the 1950 and 1960 county age distributions reported in the U.S. Census and sum the appropriate county distributions for each SEA. Subtract from each SEA's age distribution the age distribution of out-migrants to find the age distribution that did not move during the five-year period.

---

of net migrants in the 30–34 age group. An examination of the correlations between total net migrants in the 0–4 age group and those in each five-year age group between 20–44 suggested this hypothesis. The function estimated by regression methods was:

$$N_{1j} = -30.5789 + .808919(N_{7j}) \quad [R^2 = .95]$$

where N_{ij} = total net migrants in the *i*th age group in the *j*th region.

The process of transforming the estimated place-to-place flow matrices into transition matrices is straightforward. Briefly, each element of every matrix is divided by its corresponding row sum. This latter figure is also the population of the origin at the beginning of the transition period. One of the 17 transition matrices estimated for use in this study is presented in Figure 3.2.

Performance of the Simplified Interregional Cohort-Survival Model

Before generating population projections for 1980, the performance of the simplified interregional cohort-survival model was tested with 1950 and 1960 data. California's 1950 age disaggregated SEA populations were input to the model and projections of 1960's 19 SEA age distributions were derived. Summarized results of this test series appear in Table 3.1.

Despite strict assumptions with respect to the behavior of the fundamental components of population change, the model, with 1950 data as a base, predicted California's 1960 population to within 2 percent of the true total. Individual SEA forecasts provide a reasonably close fit to actual counts and a large proportion of the discrepancies between projected and observed values presumably could be reduced by an improved data base.

3.4. Forecasting with the Simplified Interregional Cohort-Survival Model

In general, the simplified interregional cohort-survival model appears to be a moderately successful tool for generating short-run projections. With inadequate information concerning migration patterns, and in spite of several strict assumptions with respect to interregional mortality and fertility rates, and interregional migration, the model generates a reasonably accurate "post-hoc" projection of California's interregional population distribution over a ten-year period. Its use for forecasting, therefore, may be justified. The results of a trial run are described in this section.

The Survivorship Matrix

For the trial forecasts reported in this section, two simplifying assumptions have been adopted: (1) the age-specific death rates

FROM SEA* \ TO SEA*	A	B	C	D	E	F	G	H	J	K	1	2	3	4	5	6	7	8	9	10
FLOWS																				
A	163399	4634	1600	622	449	3926	1214	561	260	207	518	1872	1157	821	455	217	126	37	996	13623
B	1927	25658	223	105	133	650	181	120	74	58	79	149	622	130	115	80	52	15	209	2316
C	910	225	23601	232	100	524	125	147	51	40	60	96	154	681	99	50	16	8	727	2522
D	588	215	371	12581	86	330	73	62	45	9	43	59	125	141	239	62	22	17	197	782
E	492	308	184	105	17971	726	99	124	204	53	50	41	229	71	192	581	54	18	87	999
F	3634	2199	1540	307	687	386440	3937	6541	1027	1397	247	339	1436	610	349	587	1608	144	1083	27401
G	803	311	126	61	64	2485	51179	603	103	128	39	62	162	72	42	42	173	81	83	8483
H	361	170	203	35	114	2928	720	34281	199	142	49	55	192	97	106	98	97	65	173	4097
J	275	176	101	57	213	1159	165	249	14701	169	40	33	262	76	74	270	128	23	89	1509
K	172	82	27	11	39	456	61	68	59	5931	15	12	199	23	12	26	155	10	29	509
1	454	112	151	60	55	198	56	46	24	27	8108	344	89	192	48	42	11	3	273	1311
2	693	156	126	40	38	204	63	51	22	14	174	8889	73	110	35	30	11	1	123	706
3	689	621	134	74	151	588	168	118	92	166	42	68	16677	82	97	97	64	30	94	2024
4	467	132	665	76	69	238	70	78	51	15	120	94	103	12022	63	44	23	9	462	961
5	497	236	179	266	261	364	80	108	59	26	52	62	133	98	11481	167	23	13	175	1204
6	289	198	89	61	627	527	93	125	270	41	59	54	179	73	164	11978	43	11	84	719
7	130	103	36	8	42	747	139	118	69	161	16	15	69	39	35	52	8724	6	58	968
8	43	44	23	22	37	291	315	159	33	13	7	4	39	15	25	29	27	3880	7	462
9	565	160	709	151	75	407	97	131	63	23	172	101	129	537	154	69	27	12	12804	1494
10	23998	8056	5782	1333	2283	77089	21760	10907	2637	2693	1614	1292	4588	2157	2009	1689	2409	549	2248	11210907
PROPORTIONS																				
A	0.8307	0.0236	0.0081	0.0032	0.0023	0.0200	0.0062	0.0029	0.0013	0.0011	0.0026	0.0095	0.0059	0.0042	0.0023	0.0011	0.0006	0.0002	0.0051	0.0693
B	0.0586	0.7800	0.0068	0.0032	0.0040	0.0198	0.0055	0.0036	0.0022	0.0018	0.0024	0.0045	0.0189	0.0040	0.0035	0.0024	0.0016	0.0005	0.0064	0.0704
C	0.0300	0.0074	0.7772	0.0076	0.0033	0.0173	0.0041	0.0048	0.0017	0.0013	0.0020	0.0032	0.0051	0.0224	0.0033	0.0016	0.0005	0.0003	0.0239	0.0830
D	0.0366	0.0134	0.0231	0.7840	0.0054	0.0206	0.0045	0.0039	0.0028	0.0006	0.0027	0.0037	0.0078	0.0088	0.0149	0.0039	0.0014	0.0011	0.0123	0.0487
E	0.0218	0.0136	0.0081	0.0046	0.7956	0.0321	0.0044	0.0055	0.0090	0.0023	0.0022	0.0018	0.0101	0.0031	0.0085	0.0257	0.0024	0.0008	0.0039	0.0442
F	0.0087	0.0050	0.0035	0.0007	0.0016	0.8749	0.0089	0.0148	0.0023	0.0032	0.0006	0.0008	0.0033	0.0014	0.0008	0.0013	0.0036	0.0003	0.0025	0.0620
G	0.0123	0.0048	0.0019	0.0009	0.0010	0.0382	0.7861	0.0093	0.0016	0.0020	0.0006	0.0010	0.0025	0.0011	0.0006	0.0006	0.0027	0.0012	0.0013	0.1303
H	0.0082	0.0038	0.0046	0.0008	0.0026	0.0663	0.0163	0.7759	0.0045	0.0032	0.0011	0.0012	0.0043	0.0022	0.0024	0.0022	0.0022	0.0015	0.0039	0.0927
J	0.0139	0.0089	0.0051	0.0029	0.0108	0.0586	0.0083	0.0126	0.7436	0.0085	0.0020	0.0017	0.0133	0.0038	0.0037	0.0137	0.0065	0.0012	0.0045	0.0763
K	0.0218	0.0104	0.0034	0.0014	0.0049	0.0578	0.0077	0.0086	0.0075	0.7511	0.0019	0.0015	0.0252	0.0029	0.0015	0.0033	0.0196	0.0013	0.0037	0.0645
1	0.0391	0.0097	0.0130	0.0052	0.0047	0.0171	0.0048	0.0040	0.0021	0.0023	0.6987	0.0296	0.0077	0.0165	0.0041	0.0036	0.0009	0.0003	0.0235	0.1130
2	0.0600	0.0135	0.0109	0.0035	0.0033	0.0176	0.0055	0.0044	0.0019	0.0012	0.0151	0.7690	0.0063	0.0095	0.0030	0.0026	0.0010	0.0001	0.0106	0.0611
3	0.0312	0.0281	0.0061	0.0034	0.0068	0.0266	0.0076	0.0053	0.0042	0.0075	0.0019	0.0031	0.7554	0.0037	0.0044	0.0044	0.0029	0.0014	0.0043	0.0917
4	0.0296	0.0084	0.0422	0.0048	0.0044	0.0151	0.0044	0.0049	0.0032	0.0010	0.0076	0.0060	0.0065	0.7627	0.0040	0.0028	0.0015	0.0006	0.0293	0.0610
5	0.0321	0.0152	0.0116	0.0172	0.0169	0.0235	0.0052	0.0070	0.0038	0.0017	0.0034	0.0040	0.0086	0.0063	0.7415	0.0108	0.0015	0.0008	0.0113	0.0778
6	0.0184	0.0126	0.0057	0.0039	0.0400	0.0336	0.0059	0.0080	0.0172	0.0026	0.0038	0.0034	0.0114	0.0047	0.0105	0.7637	0.0027	0.0007	0.0054	0.0458
7	0.0113	0.0089	0.0031	0.0007	0.0036	0.0648	0.0121	0.0102	0.0060	0.0140	0.0014	0.0013	0.0060	0.0034	0.0030	0.0045	0.7563	0.0005	0.0050	0.0839
8	0.0079	0.0080	0.0042	0.0040	0.0068	0.0532	0.0575	0.0290	0.0060	0.0024	0.0013	0.0007	0.0071	0.0027	0.0046	0.0053	0.0049	0.7087	0.0013	0.0844
9	0.0316	0.0089	0.0397	0.0084	0.0042	0.0228	0.0054	0.0073	0.0035	0.0013	0.0096	0.0056	0.0072	0.0300	0.0086	0.0039	0.0015	0.0007	0.7161	0.0836
10	0.0021	0.0007	0.0005	0.0001	0.0002	0.0068	0.0019	0.0010	0.0002	0.0002	0.0001	0.0001	0.0004	0.0002	0.0002	0.0001	0.0002	0.	0.0002	0.9846

*A = San Francisco-Oakland SMSA
B = San Jose SMSA
C = Sacramento SMSA
D = Stockton SMSA
E = Fresno SMSA
F = Los Angeles-Long Beach SMSA
G = San Diego SMSA
H = San Bernardino SMSA
J = Bakersfield SMSA
K = Santa Barbara SMSA
1 = Northern Coast SEA
2 = North Central Coast SEA
3 = South Central Coast SEA
4 = Sacramento Valley SEA
5 = North San Joaquin Valley SEA
6 = South San Joaquin Valley SEA
7 = Ventura SEA
8 = Imperial Valley SEA
9 = Sierra SEA
10 = Rest of the United States

Fig. 3.2. Age-specific migration flows and proportions between 19 California Standard Economic Areas and the rest of the United States, 30–34 year age group, 1955–1960.

TABLE 3.1. Geographic Distribution of California's 1960 Population: Projected and Observed

State Economic Area	Projected	Observed*
Metropolitan areas:		
A. San Francisco-Oakland	2,812,270	2,783,359
B. San Jose	653,953	642,315
C. Sacramento	501,979	502,778
D. Stockton	239,567	249,989
E. Fresno	354,296	365,945
F. Los Angeles-Long Beach	6,296,194	6,742,696
G. San Diego	1,090,652	1,033,011
H. San Bernardino-Riverside	794,059	809,782
J. Bakersfield	291,477	291,984
K. Santa Barbara	193,456	168,962
Metropolitan subtotal	13,227,903	13,590,821
Nonmetropolitan areas:		
1. Northern Coast	157,833	187,508
2. North Central Coast	210,916	213,265
3. South Central Coast	404,391	379,010
4. Sacramento Valley	281,162	269,621
5. North San Joaquin Valley	245,425	247,740
6. South San Joaquin Valley	273,678	258,825
7. Ventura	205,151	199,138
8. Imperial Valley	63,243	72,105
9. Sierra	319,113	299,171
Nonmetropolitan subtotal	2,160,912	2,126,383
California total	15,388,815	15,717,204

* SOURCE: U.S. Bureau of the Census. (PC(1)-6B). *General Population Characteristics* 1960, Table 27.

of the 1955–1960 time interval are going to remain constant over the projection period, and (2) the age-specific birth rates of the 1955–1960 time period are going to decline, linearly, to 1940–1945 levels by 1980.

The Migration Transition Matrices

One of the most important findings growing out of the recent empirical studies of internal migration in the United States is that geographical mobility is interrelated with a myriad of fac-

Forecasting 25

tors: socioeconomic, political, and psychological. Moreover, as in so many other dimensions of human behavior, there apparrently are no "laws" of migration. However, it appears that certain observable regularities in movement patterns may be systematically related to spatial separation and to spatial variations in economic opportunities.

In Chapter 7 we summarize the results of a recent attempt to test this hypothesis by statistically measuring the degree of association between spatial variations in economic opportunities and variations in interregional migration flows in California.[6] There it was found that spatial differentials in per capita wages and salaries, size of the labor force, and distance were significantly related to variations in migration flows between California regions. Hence for the forecasts reported here it was assumed that the migration of labor force "eligibles" in California may be forecast by an "economic opportunity" model. The selection of the variables for the model was made with one overriding constraint: the variables either must be internally generated by the growth model, or reliable forecasts of their change must be available for the projection period. Within this limitation, and drawing on the results of the migration study cited above, the following variables were selected:

(a) per capita wages and salaries;
(b) labor force "eligibles";[7] and
(c) interregional distances.

Economic studies conducted for Phase I of the California State Development Plan provide forecasts of total wages and salaries for the state and for three of its regions: San Francisco, Los Angeles, and San Diego.[8] These were decomposed into forecasts for the state's 19 SEA's by "share-of-total" trends. For example, Sacramento's share of the San Francisco Region's total wages and salaries was estimated to be:

$$WS_{SAC} = -302{,}457 + .153906(WS_{SFR}).$$

These decompositions of the Phase I wages and salaries forecasts

---

[6] Andrei Rogers, "A Regression Analysis of Interregional Migration in California," *The Review of Economics and Statistics*, forthcoming.

[7] The population in the 15–64 age group.

[8] Arthur D. Little, Inc., *Population and Economic Forecasts*, California State Development Plan, Phase I, November 1963.

were used to generate the per capita wages and salaries inputs for the forecasts.[9]

Labor force "eligibles" were internally generated by the model at each iteration. Total populations in each of the five-year age groups, within the 15–64 year range, were summed to derive each SEA's labor force eligibles.

Interregional distances were fed into the model along with other inputs. These are crude estimates of inter-SEA county seat highway mileages.

Per capita wages and salaries, labor force eligibles, and interregional distances were combined within a multiple regression framework to generate 10 equations, one for each age group. These were of the form:

$$(3.6) \quad _rp_{ij} = {}_rb_0 + {}_rb_1(WS_j) + {}_rb_2(LF_j) + {}_rb_3(D_{ij})$$

where $_rp_{ij}$ = proportion of people in the rth age group who move from i to j and into the next age group;

WS_j = per capita wages and salaries at j;

LF_j = labor force eligibles at j;

D_{ij} = distance between i and j.

Per capita wages and salaries and labor force eligibles at i were originally included but were found to be statistically insignificant. A typical example of the estimation results is presented in Table 3.2.

TABLE 3.2. MIGRATION EQUATION FOR ESTIMATING THE 25–29 AGE GROUP TRANSITION PROPORTIONS

Coefficient of Multiple Determination 0.57900
Multiple Correlation Coefficient 0.76092
Significance of Multiple Correlation $F(3,338) = 154.950$

Variable	Coefficient	Standard error of coefficients	Student's t	Sig. level
(Constant)	2.67588E-03			
WS_j	1.02182E-05	2.25766E-06	4.52603	0.00000
LF_j	7.69403E-09	7.20844E-10	10.67364	0.00000
D_{ij}	−2.99496E-05	2.73951E-06	−10.93246	0.00000

[9] Estimates for "the rest of the United States" were made on the basis of NPA projections reported in: National Planning Association, *National Economic Projections to 1974*, Report No. 64-3, Table 5, p. 36.

Forecasting

Ten regression equations were used to estimate the age-specific transition proportions for each iteration of the growth model. In general, these tended to overestimate the migrating component of each region's population. Thus a normalization process was incorporated into the model. This ensured that all $_rp_{ij}$ summed to a control figure, $_rp_i$, where:

$_rp_i$ = the proportion of the population of the rth age group, in the ith region, who move during a unit interval of time.

In particular, it was assumed that for each time period $(t, t+1)$:

$$_rp_i = \alpha_{ri}\left(\frac{WS_{cal}}{WS_i}\right),$$

TABLE 3.3. GEOGRAPHIC DISTRIBUTION OF CALIFORNIA'S POPULATION: 1960 AND 1980

State Economic Area	1960	1980
Metropolitan areas:		
A. San Francisco-Oakland	2,783,359	3,774,565
B. San Jose	642,315	1,637,450
C. Sacramento	502,778	1,298,393
D. Stockton	249,989	690,179
E. Fresno	365,945	731,054
F. Los Angeles-Long Beach	6,742,696	9,953,946
G. San Diego	1,033,011	2,099,328
H. San Bernardino-Riverside	809,782	1,277,072
J. Bakersfield	291,984	639,880
K. Santa Barbara	168,962	1,102,813
Metropolitan subtotal	13,590,821	23,204,680
Nonmetropolitan areas:		
1. Northern Coast	187,508	312,491
2. North Central Coast	213,265	494,396
3. South Central Coast	379,010	669,914
4. Sacramento Valley	269,621	771,483
5. North San Joaquin Valley	247,740	566,407
6. South San Joaquin Valley	258,825	536,867
7. Ventura	199,138	771,572
8. Imperial Valley	72,105	488,423
9. Sierra	299,171	545,290
Nonmetropolitan subtotal	2,126,383	5,156,843
California total	15,717,204	28,361,523

where α_{ri} = a constant calibrated on the basis of 1955–1960 data;
WS_{cal} = California's per capita wages and salaries;
WS_i = per capita wages and salaries for the ith region.

For age groups outside of the 15–64 age group the following assumptions generated the relevant migration transition matrices:

1. The migration of younger age groups (0–14) is a linear function of migration in the middle age groups (20–44).
2. The migration of the elderly is a function of amenities such as climate and is assumed to have a constant transition pattern, i.e., 1955–1960 migration transition matrices were used.

Review of Findings

If present demographic and economic trends continue, California's total 1980 population will exceed 28 million people.

TABLE 3.4. AGE COMPOSITION OF CALIFORNIA'S POPULATION: 1960 AND 1980

Age Group	1960 Population	1960 Percent	1980 Population	1980 Percent
All ages	15,717,204	100.00	28,361,523	100.00
0–4	1,745,799	11.11	3,146,248	11.09
5–9	1,600,152	10.18	2,673,382	9.43
10–14	1,417,744	9.02	2,358,376	8.31
15–19	1,096,022	6.97	2,297,139	8.10
20–24	983,660	6.26	2,452,693	8.65
25–29	1,016,083	6.46	2,488,055	8.77
30–34	1,114,137	7.09	2,314,840	8.16
35–39	1,205,361	7.67	1,828,831	6.45
40–44	1,072,637	6.82	1,477,906	5.21
45–49	972,021	6.18	1,356,150	4.78
50–54	821,270	5.23	1,357,300	4.79
55–59	706,922	4.50	1,322,421	4.66
60–64	589,192	3.75	1,076,706	3.80
65–69	512,551	3.26	862,745	3.04
70–74	398,164	2.53	622,367	2.19
75–79	257,047	1.64	415,758	1.47
80–84	132,039	.84	228,796	.81
85+	76,403	.49	81,810	.29

Forecasting

More than 80 percent of California's total population will reside in the state's metropolitan areas, and the population will continue to be concentrated in two major regions: the Bay Area, centered around San Francisco, and the southern megalopolis spreading outwards from Los Angeles. These two regions accounted for over 60 percent of the state's population in 1960 and should absorb about 40 percent of the projected population increase during the 1960 to 1980 period. The projected growth of California's SEA populations is summarized in Table 3.3. Age-specific detail is provided in Table 3.4. Data on net migration may be found in Table 3.5.

TABLE 3.5. GEOGRAPHIC DISTRIBUTION OF NET MIGRATION IN CALIFORNIA: 1955–1960 AND 1960–1980

State Economic Area	1955–1960	1960–1980
Metropolitan areas:		
A. San Francisco-Oakland	55,059	230,267
B. San Jose	144,800	660,172
C. Sacramento	77,507	535,427
D. Stockton	471	311,269
E. Fresno	9,559	213,085
F. Los Angeles-Long Beach	480,335	1,238,453
G. San Diego	163,477	600,691
H. San Bernardino-Riverside	111,082	197,685
J. Bakersfield	1,674	194,008
K. Santa Barbara	43,013	748,094
Metropolitan subtotal	1,086,977	4,929,151
Nonmetropolitan areas:		
1. Northern Coast	−3,205	47,884
2. North Central Coast	19,368	202,477
3. South Central Coast	39,281	155,355
4. Sacramento Valley	21,319	365,967
5. North San Joaquin Valley	1,082	210,864
6. South San Joaquin Valley	−771	175,069
7. Ventura	29,407	419,672
8. Imperial Valley	−7,103	324,956
9. Sierra	23,445	143,614
Nonmetropolitan subtotal	122,823	2,045,858
California total	1,209,800	6,975,009

3.5. References

[1] Rogers, Andrei, "A Regression Analysis of Interregional Migration in California," *The Review of Economics and Statistics*, forthcoming.

[2] ———, "Experiments with a Matrix Model of Population Growth and Distribution," *Proceedings of the Fourth Annual International Conference on Operations Research*, Cambridge, August 1966.

[3] ———, "Sensitivity Tests of a Model of Population Growth in California Regions," *Papers of the Regional Science Association*, Western Section Proceedings, Santa Barbara, January 1966, pp. 180–195.

[4] ———, *Projected Population Growth in California Regions*, Center for Planning and Development Research, University of California, Berkeley, December 1965.

[5] ———, *An Analysis of Interregional Migration in California*, Center for Planning and Development Research, University of California, Berkeley, December 1965.

4 ESTIMATION

4.1. Introduction

A common constraint in interregional population analysis and forecasting is the absence of reliable data concerning the behavior of the fundamental components of population change, particularly in- and out-migration. We can identify two classes of estimation problems, each associated with a particular level of data availability:

(1) Data on births, deaths, and migration are available, but only over an n *unit time interval*. It is desired to estimate the corresponding data for an "average" *single unit time interval*. We define this estimation problem as *estimation by temporal decomposition*.

(2) Data on births, deaths, and migration are unavailable, but a time series of interregional population distributions is available. It is desired to estimate birth, death, and migration data using the time series. We define this estimation problem as *estimation on the basis of distributional data*.

4.2. Estimation by Temporal Decomposition

The problem of decomposing a growth operator, G, which defines a growth regime during an n unit time interval, into the corresponding "average" growth operator for a single unit time interval, is equivalent to the problem of finding a matrix P such that

$$(4.1) \qquad P^n = G.$$

A convenient solution method is to find a collinearity transformation of G such that

$$(4.2) \qquad G = NDN^{-1},$$

where D is a diagonal matrix, and N is a suitably constructed nonsingular square matrix of the same order as G. Such a transformation enables one to examine a number of polynomial functions of G. For example,

$$\begin{aligned} G^2 &= (NDN^{-1})(NDN^{-1}) \\ &= ND(N^{-1}N)DN^{-1} \\ &= ND^2N^{-1}. \end{aligned}$$

Using the associative property of matrix multiplication, the above argument may be extended to higher powers and thus to polynomial functions of G:

(4.3) $$f(G) = Nf(D)N^{-1},$$

where $f(\cdot)$ is a polynomial function.

Since the temporal decomposition problem, in effect, is to find $G^{1/n}$, we may use (4.3) to establish the relationship:

(4.4) $$G^{1/n} = ND^{1/n}N^{-1}.$$

A well-known result in matrix algebra establishes that for a G with distinct characteristic roots, a solution for D in (4.2), is a diagonal matrix with nonzero entries equal to the characteristic roots of the determinental equation:[1]

(4.5) $$\|G - \lambda I\| = 0.$$

Moreover, it is also established that the columns of N are the characteristic vectors which correspond to the characteristic roots of (4.5).[2] A unique solution does not exist; however, any solution will satisfy (4.4). One such solution may be constructed by using the cofactors of the first row of $[G - \lambda_i I]$ for the ith column of N.

At this point the two-region growth process of (2.5) may serve to clarify the discussion.

Recall that the characteristic roots of the growth operator in (2.5) are $\lambda_1 = 1.0802$ and $\lambda_2 = 1.0080$. Hence

$$D = \begin{bmatrix} 1.0802 & 0 \\ 0 & 1.0080 \end{bmatrix}.$$

The two cofactors of the first row of $[G - \lambda_1 I]$ are

$$n_{11} = -.0135,$$
$$n_{21} = -.0627.$$

---

[1] R. A. Frazer, W. J. Duncan, and A. R. Collar, *Elementary Matrices* (Cambridge: Cambridge University Press, 7th reprinting, 1963), pp. 64–70.
[2] *Ibid.*

Estimation

Analogously, for $[G - \lambda_2 I]$ we have

$$n_{12} = .0587$$
$$n_{22} = -.0627.$$

Thus we may assemble the matrix

$$N = \begin{bmatrix} -.0135 & .0587 \\ -.0627 & -.0627 \end{bmatrix}$$

and find its inverse

$$N^{-1} = \begin{bmatrix} -13.8504 & -12.9668 \\ 13.8504 & -2.9821 \end{bmatrix}.$$

As a check on our arithmetic, it is a simple matter to compute NDN^{-1} and confirm that the result is indeed the matrix G.

With the collinear transform of G we now are in a position to find $G^{1/5}$. The first step is to derive $D^{1/5}$. Since D is a diagonal matrix, we need only to find the fifth roots of its nonzero elements:

$$D^{1/5} = \begin{bmatrix} 1.0155 & 0 \\ 0 & 1.0016 \end{bmatrix}.$$

Recalling (4.4), we have:

$$P = G^{1/5} = ND^{1/5}N^{-1}$$
$$= \begin{bmatrix} -.0135 & .0587 \\ -.0627 & -.0627 \end{bmatrix} \begin{bmatrix} 1.0155 & 0 \\ 0 & 1.0016 \end{bmatrix}$$
$$\begin{bmatrix} -13.8504 & -12.9668 \\ 13.8504 & -2.9821 \end{bmatrix} = \begin{bmatrix} 1.0042 & .0024 \\ .0121 & 1.0129 \end{bmatrix}.$$

By applying the one-year growth operator, P, to the interregional distribution in 1955, $\mathbf{w}^{(1955)}$, we can derive an estimate of the 1956 interregional distribution, $\mathbf{w}^{(1956)}$:

$$\begin{bmatrix} 13408 \\ 154201 \end{bmatrix} = \begin{bmatrix} 1.0042 & .0024 \\ .0121 & 1.0129 \end{bmatrix} \begin{bmatrix} 12988 \\ 152082 \end{bmatrix}$$
$$= \begin{bmatrix} 13043 + & 365 \\ 157 + & 154044 \end{bmatrix}$$

and, recursively, the time series of interregional distributions presented in Table 4.1.

Moreover, the off-diagonal proportions allow us to estimate interregional flows (Table 4.2) and, by subtracting unity from the diagonal elements, we have an estimate of the rate of natural

TABLE 4.1. Interregional Distributions Generated by a Constant Growth Operator: California and the Rest of the United States: 1955–1960

Region	1955	1956	1957	1958	1959	1960
California	12,988	13,408	13,834	14,267	14,707	15,155
Rest of the United States	152,082	154,201	156,352	158,536	160,754	163,006
Total	165,070	167,609	170,186	172,803	175,461	178,161

Estimation

TABLE 4.2. INTERREGIONAL MIGRATION TRANSITION
MATRIX: 1955–1956 (in 000's)

From \ To	California	U.S.	1955 Total population
California	12,623 (.9879)	157 (.0121)	12,988 (1.0000)
Rest of the United States	365 (.0024)	151,717 (.9976)	152,082 (1.0000)

increase in each region. If we assume that the ratio between the number of births and the number of deaths that existed for the five-year period also holds for each one-year period, we may decompose the natural increase figure into total births and deaths. Table 4.3 illustrates some of these results.

4.3. Estimation on the Basis of Distributional Data

Consider, next, the problem of estimating a growth operator for an interregional system in the absence of data on births, deaths, and migration. For ease of exposition, let us adopt the two-region example discussed above and assume that the growth operator remains unchanged over two sequential time intervals. We have then:[3]

$$\begin{bmatrix} w_1^{(t+1)} \\ w_2^{(t+1)} \end{bmatrix} = \begin{bmatrix} g_{11} & g_{21} \\ g_{12} & g_{22} \end{bmatrix} \begin{bmatrix} w_1^{(t)} \\ w_2^{(t)} \end{bmatrix}$$

and

$$\begin{bmatrix} w_1^{(t+2)} \\ w_2^{(t+2)} \end{bmatrix} = \begin{bmatrix} g_{11} & g_{21} \\ g_{12} & g_{22} \end{bmatrix} \begin{bmatrix} w_1^{(t+1)} \\ w_2^{(t+1)} \end{bmatrix}.$$

Assume that the w's have been observed and therefore are known, but that the matrix growth operator, G, is unknown and has to be estimated solely on the basis of the observed w's. We have, then, a problem in the solution of a system of 4 equations in 4 unknowns. Thus, for example, given $\mathbf{w}^{(1955)}$, $\mathbf{w}^{(1956)}$, and

---

[3] In order to carry on with notation that is consistent with that found in other chapters of this monograph, we denote the annual growth operator by G and not by P as in the previous section. There we needed to distinguish between two different growth operators; in the rest of this chapter we do not.

TABLE 4.3. Components of Population Change in California and the Rest of the United States: 1955–1956

(1) Region	(2) 1955 Population (000's)	(3) Births 1955–56 (000's)	(4) Deaths 1955–56 (000's)	(5) Net migration 1955–56 (000's)	(6) Crude birth rate	(7) Crude death rate	(8) Crude net migration rate	(9) 1956 Population (000's)
California	12,988	315	103	208	0.0242	0.0079	0.0160	13,408
Rest of the United States	152,082	3,761	1,434	−208	0.0247	0.0094	−0.0014	154,201
Total	165,070	4,076	1,537	—	—	—	—	167,609

Estimation

$\mathbf{w}^{(1957)}$ of Table 4.1, and assuming that the equations are independent, we may solve the system described below and find the matrix growth operator G:

$$12988g_{11} + 152082g_{21} = 13408$$
$$12988g_{12} + 152082g_{22} = 154201$$
$$13408g_{11} + 154201g_{21} = 13834$$
$$13408g_{12} + 154201g_{22} = 156352$$

whence,

$$g_{11} = 1.0042 \quad g_{21} = .0024$$
$$g_{12} = .0121 \quad g_{22} = 1.0129.$$

Notice that by solving the equation system we have extracted migration information from data only on interregional population distributions.

We now consider the more general problem of estimating an operator G which, when applied to the vector $\mathbf{w}^{(1955)}$, reproduces, as accurately as possible, the entire distributional time series in Table 4.1. If, as before, we assume that G does not change during the five-year interval, we have a system of 10 equations in 4 unknowns, and a criterion of "goodness-of-fit" needs to be introduced for a unique solution to exist. Three have been suggested in the literature: (1) the unrestricted least-squares estimator;[4] (2) the minimum absolute deviations estimator;[5] and (3) the restricted least-squares estimator.[6] The first adopts the well-known estimation technique traditionally used in regression analysis; the latter two require a mathematical programming formulation.

---

[4] George A. Miller, "Finite Markov Processes in Psychology," *Psychometrika*, Vol. 17 (1952), 149–167; A. Madansky, "Least Squares Estimation in Finite Markov Processes," *Psychometrika*, 25 (1959), 137–144.

[5] W. D. Fisher, "A Note on Curve Fitting with Minimum Deviations by Linear Programming," *Journal of the American Statistical Association*, 56 (1961), 359–362; Harvey M. Wagner, "Linear Programming Techniques for Regression Analysis," *Journal of the American Statistical Association*, 54 (1959), 206–212.

[6] G. G. Judge and T. Takayama, "Inequality Restrictions in Regression Analysis," *Journal of the American Statistical Association*, 61 (1966), 166–181; Henry Theil and Guido Rey, "A Quadratic Programming Approach to the Estimation of Transition Probabilities," *Management Science*, 12 (1966), 714–721.

The Unrestricted Least-Squares Estimator

We begin by defining our statistical model. Assume that the observed vectors, **w**, denoting the population in each of m regions over n years, are generated by the linear model

(4.6) $$\mathbf{w}^{(t+1)} = G\mathbf{w}^{(t)} + \boldsymbol{\epsilon}^{(t)}$$

where $\boldsymbol{\epsilon}^{(t)}$ is a $(mn \times 1)$ vector of error terms. Expressing (4.6) in the more familiar linear regression form, we have:

(4.7) $$\mathbf{y} = X\mathbf{g} + \boldsymbol{\epsilon}$$

where, for our two-region example,

$$\mathbf{y} = \begin{bmatrix} \mathbf{y}_1 \\ \mathbf{y}_2 \end{bmatrix} \quad \mathbf{g} = \begin{bmatrix} \mathbf{g}_1 \\ \mathbf{g}_2 \end{bmatrix} \quad \boldsymbol{\epsilon} = \begin{bmatrix} \boldsymbol{\epsilon}_1 \\ \boldsymbol{\epsilon}_2 \end{bmatrix} \quad X = \begin{bmatrix} X_1 & 0 \\ 0 & X_2 \end{bmatrix} \quad X_1 = X_2$$

or, more specifically,

$$\underset{2n \times 1}{\mathbf{y}} = \begin{bmatrix} w_1^{(t+1)} \\ w_1^{(t+2)} \\ \cdot \\ \cdot \\ w_1^{(t+n)} \\ \hline w_2^{(t+1)} \\ w_2^{(t+2)} \\ \cdot \\ \cdot \\ w_2^{(t+n)} \end{bmatrix} \quad \underset{2^2 \times 1}{\mathbf{g}} = \begin{bmatrix} g_{11} \\ g_{21} \\ \hline g_{12} \\ g_{22} \end{bmatrix}, \quad \underset{2n \times 1}{\boldsymbol{\epsilon}} = \begin{bmatrix} \epsilon_{11} \\ \epsilon_{12} \\ \cdot \\ \cdot \\ \epsilon_{1n} \\ \hline \epsilon_{21} \\ \epsilon_{22} \\ \cdot \\ \cdot \\ \epsilon_{2n} \end{bmatrix}$$

and

$$\underset{2n \times 2^2}{X} = \begin{bmatrix} w_1^{(t)} & w_2^{(t)} & 0 & 0 \\ w_1^{(t+1)} & w_2^{(t+1)} & 0 & 0 \\ \cdot & \cdot & \cdot & \cdot \\ \cdot & \cdot & \cdot & \cdot \\ w_1^{(t+n-1)} & w_2^{(t+n-1)} & 0 & 0 \\ \hline 0 & 0 & w_1^{(t)} & w_2^{(t)} \\ 0 & 0 & w_1^{(t+1)} & w_2^{(t+1)} \\ \cdot & \cdot & \cdot & \cdot \\ \cdot & \cdot & \cdot & \cdot \\ 0 & 0 & w_1^{(t+n-1)} & w_2^{(t+n-1)} \end{bmatrix}$$

Recalling that the least-squares estimator of **g** is one which minimizes the sum of squared deviations of observed from predicted values, we minimize

Estimation

(4.8) $\quad S = \sum (y_i - \hat{y}_i)^2 = [\mathbf{y} - X\mathbf{g}]'[\mathbf{y} - X\mathbf{g}]$

with respect to **g** and find

(4.9) $\quad\quad\quad\quad \hat{\mathbf{g}} = (X'X)^{-1}X'\mathbf{y}.$

Applying (4.9) to our two-region example, we once again find the growth matrix G:

$$\hat{G} = \begin{bmatrix} \hat{g}_{11} & \hat{g}_{21} \\ \hat{g}_{12} & \hat{g}_{22} \end{bmatrix} = \begin{bmatrix} 1.0042 & .0024 \\ .0121 & 1.0129 \end{bmatrix}.$$

Unrestricted least-squares estimation leaves unresolved a serious problem in the estimation of growth operators. This is the possible entry of negative elements into G. These, of course, are by definition inadmissible estimates. To cope with this problem, Telser[7] has suggested a method whereby negative elements are set equal to zero or unity and the matrix adjusted to compensate for this change. Such a procedure is unsatisfactory, however, since it leads to extensive iterative computations when the number of inadmissible estimates is large. Failure to exhaust all possible alternatives in the assignment of admissible extreme values may lead to estimates which do not minimize the sum of squares of error. A more efficient approach is to incorporate a nonnegativity constraint in the estimation process. Such a restriction may be introduced by mathematical programming formulations of the estimation problem.

The Minimum Absolute Deviations Estimator

The minimum absolute deviations estimator finds the vector of parameter estimates which minimizes the sum of the *absolute values* of the deviations between observed and predicted values. That is, it derives the vector **g** which minimizes

(4.10) $\quad\quad\quad S = \sum |y_i - \hat{y}_i| = |\mathbf{y} - X\mathbf{g}|'\mathbf{1},$

subject to the constraints

(4.11) $\quad\quad\quad\quad \mathbf{y} = X\mathbf{g} + \boldsymbol{\epsilon}$
(4.12) $\quad\quad\quad\quad \mathbf{g} \geq \mathbf{0}.$

To transform (4.10) into a form that is solvable by linear programming methods, we express each ϵ_i as the difference of

---

[7] Lester G. Telser, "Least Squares Estimates of Transition Probabilities," in *Measurement in Economics*, F. Christ (ed.), (Palo Alto, California: Stanford University Press, 1963), pp. 272–292.

two nonnegative variables u_i and v_i. Thus we now seek the vector **g** which minimizes

(4.13) $$S = [\mathbf{u} + \mathbf{v}]'\mathbf{1}$$

subject to the constraints

(4.14) $$\mathbf{y} = X\mathbf{g} + \boldsymbol{\epsilon} = X\mathbf{g} + [I, -I]\begin{bmatrix}\mathbf{u}\\\mathbf{v}\end{bmatrix}$$

(4.15) $$\mathbf{g}, \mathbf{u}, \mathbf{v} \geq 0.$$

The problem can be solved by using the simplex algorithm on the tableau presented in Table 4.4. Since in (4.14) the vectors **u** and **v** are linearly dependent, elements of one or the other, but not both, will enter the optimal solution.[8]

TABLE 4.4. Linear Programming Tableau for Finding the Minimum Absolute Deviations Estimate

B	0'	0' ... 0'	1'	1' ... 1'	1'	1' ... 1'
	g'_1	$g'_2 \ldots g'_r$	u'_1	$u'_2 \ldots u'_r$	v'_1	$v'_2 \ldots v'_r$
y_1	X_1		I_n		$-I_n$	
y_2		X_2		I_n		$-I_n$
...		...		...		...
y_r		X_r		I_n		$-I_n$

Expressing the two-region example of Table 4.1 in the form of a simplex tableau, we have Table 4.5, and applying the simplex algorithm we find, once again, the estimate of G to be:[9]

$$\hat{G} = \begin{bmatrix} 1.0042 & .0024 \\ .0121 & 1.0129 \end{bmatrix}.$$

---

[8] If a particular u_i and v_i were both strictly positive, with $u_i > v_i$ say, the solution could not be optimal since it would be possible to find a smaller value for S in (4.13) by replacing u_i by $u_i - v_i$ and setting the original v_i equal to zero.

[9] In theory, the alternative estimates of G, for the synthetically generated interregional population distributions in Table 4.1, must be identical. In practice, however, rounding errors introduce slight differences in the third and fourth decimal places.

Estimation 41

TABLE 4.5. LINEAR PROGRAMMING TABLEAU FOR THE TWO-REGION EXAMPLE

	0	0	0	0	1	1	1	1	1	1	1	1	1	1	1	1	1	1	1	1	1	1	1	1
B	g_{11}	g_{21}	g_{12}	g_{22}	u_{11}	u_{12}	u_{13}	u_{14}	u_{15}	u_{21}	u_{22}	u_{23}	u_{24}	u_{25}	v_{11}	v_{12}	v_{13}	v_{14}	v_{15}	v_{21}	v_{22}	v_{23}	v_{24}	v_{25}
13,408	12,988	152,082			1										-1									
13,834	13,408	154,201				1										-1								
14,267	13,834	156,352					1										-1							
14,707	14,267	158,536						1										-1						
15,155	14,707	160,754							1										-1					
154,201			12,988	152,082						1										-1				
156,352			13,408	154,201							1										-1			
158,536			13,834	156,352								1										-1		
160,754			14,267	158,536									1										-1	
163,006			14,707	160,754										1										-1

The Restricted Least-Squares Estimator

Recall the unrestricted least-squares estimation problem. There we sought a vector **g** which minimized

(4.16) $\quad S = [\mathbf{y} - X\mathbf{g}]'[\mathbf{y} - X\mathbf{g}] = \mathbf{y}'\mathbf{y} - 2\mathbf{g}'X'\mathbf{y} + \mathbf{g}'X'X\mathbf{g}.$

No constraints on **g** were imposed. To introduce the restriction that all $g_{ij} \geq 0$, we may formulate the estimation problem as:

Find the vector **g** that minimizes (4.16) subject to the constraints:

(4.17) $\quad\quad\quad\quad\quad \mathbf{g} \geq \mathbf{0}.$

Since (4.16) is a quadratic form in **g** and the constraints are linear, we have a problem in quadratic programming. By making use of the duality theorem for quadratic programs and the "equivalence" theorem for nonlinear programming,[10] we may formulate the following primal-dual problem:

Find the vector **g** that maximizes

(4.18) $\quad\quad [X'\mathbf{y} - (X'X)\mathbf{g}]'\mathbf{g} = -\mathbf{g}'\mathbf{v} \leq 0$

subject to

(4.19) $\quad\quad\quad\quad (X'X)\mathbf{g} - \mathbf{v} = X'\mathbf{y}$
(4.20) $\quad\quad\quad\quad\quad\quad \mathbf{g}, \mathbf{v} \geq \mathbf{0}.$

The above quadratic programming problem may be solved by a slightly modified simplex algorithm developed by Wolfe.[11] The tableau for this problem appears in Table 4.6.

Expressing the data in Table 4.1 in the form of the tableau of Table 4.6, we obtain Table 4.7, and applying Wolfe's algorithm we once again derive the following estimate of G:

$$\hat{G} = \begin{bmatrix} 1.0042 & .0024 \\ .0121 & 1.0129 \end{bmatrix}.$$

In this section we have demonstrated that it is possible to estimate the schedule of interregional population growth and migration solely on the basis of data on interregional population

---

[10] Thomas L. Saaty and Joseph Bram, *Nonlinear Mathematics* (New York: McGraw-Hill, 1964), pp. 113–133.

[11] Phillip Wolfe, "The Simplex Method for Quadratic Programming," *Econometrica*, 27 (1959), 382–398.

Estimation

TABLE 4.6. Quadratic Programming Tableau for Finding the Restricted Least-Squares Estimate

B	$0'$ g'_1	$0'$ g'_2	$\ldots 0'$ $\ldots g'_r$	$0'$ v'_1	$0'$ v'_2	$\ldots 0'$ $\ldots v'_r$
$X'_1 y_1$	$X'_1 X_1$			$-I$		
$X'_2 y_2$		$X'_2 X_2$			$-I$	
$\ldots$			$\ldots$			$\ldots$
$X'_r y_r$			$X'_r X_r$			$-I$

distributions over several time periods. Three alternative estimators were defined and illustrated with a synthetically generated two-region population. Problems may arise, however, when observed, rather than artificial, data are used. The assumption of a constant growth operator, for example, becomes less viable as the number of time periods is increased. This assumption may lead to a poor fit and force a large number of error terms into the solution basis, thereby forcing out some of the elements of the operator G. Another problem occurs when the regions differ considerably in size. In such instances an error in estimating a g_{ij} associated with a small region should not, perhaps, have the same weight as an identical error associated with the estimation of a g_{ij} associated with a large region. Hence, a weighted estimation procedure may need to be employed.

4.4. References

[1] Ashar, V. and T. D. Wallace, "A Sampling Study of Minimum Absolute Deviations Estimator," *Operations Research*, 11 (1963), 747–751.

[2] Fisher, W. D., "A Note on Curve Fitting with Minimum Deviations by Linear Programming," *Journal American Statistical Association*, 56 (1961), 359–362.

[3] Judge, G. G. and T. Takayama, "Inequality Restrictions in Regression Analysis," *Journal American Statistical Association*, 61 (1966), 166–181.

[4] Karst, O. J., "Linear Curve Fitting Using Least Deviations," *Journal American Statistical Association*, 53 (1958), 118–132.

[5] Lee, T. C., G. G. Judge, and T. Takayama, "On Estimating

TABLE 4.7. QUADRATIC PROGRAMMING TABLEAU FOR THE TWO-REGION EXAMPLE

B	0	0	0	0	0	0	0	0
	g_{11}	g_{21}	g_{12}	g_{22}	v_1	v_2	v_3	v_4
989,708,408	959,685,302	10,831,783,782	0	0	−1			
11,170,821,896	10,831,783,782	122,328,342,841	0	0		−1		
10,983,123,788	0	0	959,685,302	10,831,783,782			−1	
124,037,414,574	0	0	10,831,783,782	122,328,342,841				−1

the Transition Probabilities of a Markov Process," *Journal of Farm Economics*, 43 (1965), 742–762.
[6] Madansky, A., "Least Squares Estimation in Finite Markov Process," *Psychometrika*, 25 (1959), 137–144.
[7] Miller, George A., "Finite Markov Processes in Psychology," *Psychometrika*, 17 (1952), 149–167.
[8] Rogers, Andrei and Robert Miller, "Estimating a Matrix Population Growth Operator from Distributional Time Series," *Annals of the Association of American Geographers*, forthcoming.
[9] ———, "A Note on the Temporal Decomposition of Interpoint Transition Matrices," *Journal of Regional Science*, 6 (1966), 53–56.
[10] ———, "Matrix Analysis of Interregional Population Growth and Distribution," *Papers of the Regional Science Association*, 18, VIth European Congress, Vienna, August 1966, forthcoming.
[11] Telser, Lester G., "Least Squares Estimates of Transition Probabilities," in *Measurement in Economics*, F. Christ (ed.) (Palo Alto, California: Stanford University Press, 1963), pp. 272–292.
[12] Theil, Henry and Guido Rey, "A Quadratic Programming Approach to the Estimation of Transition Probabilities," *Management Science*, 12 (1966), 714 721.
[13] Wagner, Harvey M., "Linear Programming Techniques for Regression Analysis," *Journal of the American Statistical Association*, 54 (1959), 206–212.

5 STABILITY

5.1. Introduction

In Chapter 2 we outlined the fundamental matrix model of population growth and distribution. A matrix operator, G, was defined which if applied to a population vector, $\mathbf{w}^{(t)}$, "grew" it to the population vector of the subsequent time period, $\mathbf{w}^{(t+1)}$. Consider now the population projection that is generated by an unchanging regime of growth, G. Since

$$\mathbf{w}^{(t+1)} = G\mathbf{w}^{(t)},$$

and

$$\mathbf{w}^{(t+2)} = G\mathbf{w}^{(t+1)},$$

by substitution,

$$\mathbf{w}^{(t+2)} = G^2\mathbf{w}^{(t)},$$

and, in general,

(5.1) $$\mathbf{w}^{(t+n)} = G^n\mathbf{w}^{(t)}.$$

For example, to forecast the 1980 population of our two regions in Table 2.1 we merely solve:

$$\mathbf{w}^{(1980)} = G^5\mathbf{w}^{(1955)}$$

$$= \begin{bmatrix} 1.1211 & .0756 \\ .3735 & 1.3903 \end{bmatrix} \begin{bmatrix} 12988 \\ 152082 \end{bmatrix} = \begin{bmatrix} 26058 \\ 216291 \end{bmatrix}.$$

It is interesting to notice the gradual process of stabilization of G as we go on to higher powers. For example,

$$G^{30} = \begin{bmatrix} 2.9298 & 1.5572 \\ 7.6878 & 8.4719 \end{bmatrix}$$

and

$$G^{60} = \begin{bmatrix} 20.5550 & 17.7544 \\ 87.6536 & 83.7438 \end{bmatrix}.$$

A glance at the elements of G^{30} and G^{60} suggests that the columns of G^n appear to be stabilizing around a common vector, as n is increased. As a test for stability, we may compute the ratios of corresponding elements of successive powers of G. For example, g_{11} of G^{61} is 22.1101 which divided by the g_{11} of G^{60} yields $22.1101/20.5550 = 1.0757$. Applying this operation to every element (i, j) produces the matrix L^{61}:

$$L^{61} = \begin{bmatrix} 1.0757 & 1.0814 \\ 1.0814 & 1.0800 \end{bmatrix}.$$

The elements of L are not identical, but appear to be converging toward a common limit. Raising G to higher powers will demonstrate that this indeed is the case and will yield a limiting form of L with all elements $\lambda_{ij} = 1.0802$.

Since at stability (say at time s),

(5.2) $$G^s = \lambda G^{s-1},$$

and because

$$\mathbf{w}^{(s+1)} = G\mathbf{w}^{(s)} = G^s\mathbf{w}^{(1)} = \lambda G^{s-1}\mathbf{w}^{(1)},$$

by simple substitution, we have

(5.3) $$\mathbf{w}^{(s+1)} = \lambda \mathbf{w}^{(s)}.$$

We conclude, therefore, that an interregional population vector $\mathbf{w}^{(t)}$, if subjected to an unchanging regime of growth G, will in the long run grow at a stable intrinsic rate of growth λ, where λ is the limiting value approached by the elements of the matrix L, as G is repeatedly raised to higher powers. Moreover, since λ is a scalar, we also may note that at stability the corresponding elements of successive interregional population vectors $\mathbf{w}$ differ only by a factor of λ. That is, at stability each region receives a constant share of the total population. This allocation structure we shall define as *the stable interregional population distribution* and denote it by the vector $\mathbf{v}$. Thus, in addition to (5.3), we have the following relationship at stability:

(5.4) $$\mathbf{v}^{(t+1)} = \mathbf{v}^{(t)}.$$

5.2. The Theory of Nonnegative Matrices and the Stable Interregional Population Distribution

Perron[1] was the first to prove that the characteristic root of largest absolute value of a positive matrix is both real and pos-

---

[1] Oskar Perron, "Zur Theorie der Matrizen," *Mathematische Annalen* 64 (1907), 248–263; and "Grundlagen für eine Theorie des Jakobischen Kettenbruchalgorithmus," *Mathematische Annalen*, 64 (1907), 1–76.

itive. Frobenius[2] extended this result by demonstrating that the associated characteristic vector was unique, with all components positive. He also showed that these results hold for nonnegative matrices as well if they and their powers are irreducible.[3] These results, in weaker form, have been extended to reducible nonnegative matrices.[4]

The growth operator, G, in the matrix model of population growth, is square and composed of nonnegative elements. Therefore, the Perron–Frobenius theorems hold for this class of matrices. The relevant essentials for our immediate purposes may be summarized by the following theorem:

Theorem 1: If G is a square nonnegative matrix, then there exists a nonnegative characteristic vector **x**, associated with a nonnegative characteristic root λ, which is greater or equal to the absolute value of any other characteristic root of the matrix G.

Drawing on this body of knowledge we may reformulate the problem of the stable interregional population and thereby develop a means for deriving the stable interregional distribution.

Consider the following formal problem in matrix analysis: Given a nonnegative matrix G, find a nonnegative scalar λ and a nonnegative real vector **w** such that

(5.5) $$G\mathbf{w} = \lambda \mathbf{w}$$

or

(5.6) $$(G - \lambda I)\mathbf{w} = 0.$$

---

[2] Georg F. Frobenius, "Über Matrizen aus positiven Elementen," *Sitzungsberichte der Königlich Preussischen Akademie der Wissenschaften zu Berlin* (1908), pp. 471–477; "Über Matrizen aus positiven Elementen (II)," *Sitzungsberichte* (1909), pp. 514–518; "Über Matrizen aus nicht negativen Elementen," *Sitzungsberichte* (1912), pp. 456–477; "Über zerlegbare Determinanten," *Sitzungsberichte* (1917), pp. 274–277.

[3] A matrix, A, is reducible if by simple permutation of rows and columns it can be transformed to the form:

$$A = \begin{bmatrix} B & C \\ 0 & D \end{bmatrix},$$

where B and D are square matrices and 0 is the zero matrix. If such a transformation cannot be performed, the matrix is irreducible.

[4] Samuel Karlin, *Mathematical Methods and Theory in Games, Programming, and Economics* (Reading, Mass.: Addison-Wesley, 1959), pp. 246–256.

Stability

Matrix theory informs us that for the set of m homogeneous equations in (5.6) to have a solution, the determinant of the coefficients must be equal to zero. Hence we proceed by solving the characteristic equation

(5.7) $$\|G - \lambda I\| = 0.$$

This produces a set of n roots, $\lambda_i (i = 1, 2, \ldots, n)$. Theorem 1 ensures that there exists at least one nonnegative root, λ, which is greater or equal to the absolute value of all others. It also establishes the existence of an associated positive characteristic vector, $\mathbf{w}$, whose components are all nonnegative. Hence to derive the stable interregional vector $\mathbf{v}$, we need only to apply the relation:

(5.8) $$v_i = \frac{w_i}{\sum_i w_i}.$$

5.3. The Stable Interregional Population Distribution: California and the Rest of the United States

The Interregional Components-of-Change Model

Returning to our two-region example in Table 2.1, we may easily derive the stable interregional population distribution that is implied by the growth process defined by (2.5). First solving for the characteristic roots of the characteristic equation:

$$\left\| \begin{matrix} 1.0215 - \lambda & .0127 \\ .0627 & 1.0667 - \lambda \end{matrix} \right\| = 0$$

we have

$$\lambda^2 - 2.0882\lambda + 1.0888 = 0$$

and

$$\lambda_1 = 1.0802$$
$$\lambda_2 = 1.0080.$$

The dominant root, $\lambda_1 = 1.0802$, is the intrinsic rate of growth of the interregional population at stability, and its associated characteristic vector may be found by solving (5.6) for this particular value of the root. Normalizing the elements of the resulting vector to unity [Equation (5.8)], we find the stable interregional population vector

$$\mathbf{v} = \begin{bmatrix} .1772 \\ .8228 \end{bmatrix}.$$

Table 5.1 presents these results along with recent historical distributions for comparison.

TABLE 5.1. PAST AND ASYMPTOTIC INTERREGIONAL POPULATION DISTRIBUTIONS: CALIFORNIA AND THE REST OF THE UNITED STATES

Region	1955	1960	Stable distribution
California	0.0787	0.0876	0.1772
5-year growth rate	1.2269	1.2101	$\lambda = 1.0802$
Rest of the United States	0.9213	0.9124	0.8228
5-year growth rate	1.0854	1.0758	$\lambda = 1.0802$
National 5-year growth rate	1.0954	1.0863	$\lambda = 1.0802$

The Interregional Cohort-Survival Model

The intrinsic rate of growth and the stable interregional age distribution for the growth process of Figure 2.1 may be derived by applying the method outlined above. However, for large matrices, more efficient algorithms are available.[5] Applying one such method to the growth matrix in Figure 2.1 yields an intrinsic rate of growth $\lambda = 1.2238$ and the stable interregional age vector presented in Table 5.2.

5.4. References

[1] Debreu, Gerard and I. N. Herstein, "Non-negative Square Matrices," *Econometrica*, XXI (1953), 597–607.

[2] Gantmacher, F. R., *The Theory of Matrices*, Vol. II (New York: Chelsea Publishing Co., 1959), pp. 50–112.

[3] Karlin, Samuel, *Mathematical Methods and Theory in Games, Programming, and Economics* (Reading, Mass.: Addison-Wesley, 1959), pp. 246–256.

[4] Keyfitz, Nathan, "The Intrinsic Rate of Natural Increase and the Dominant Root of the Projection Matrix," *Population Studies* (1965), 293–308.

---

[5] E. M. Murphy, "The Latent Roots of the Population Projection Matrix," *Demography*, III, 1 (1966), 259–275.

Stability

TABLE 5.2. PAST AND ASYMPTOTIC INTERREGIONAL AND INTRAREGIONAL AGE STRUCTURES: CALIFORNIA AND THE REST OF THE UNITED STATES

Age Group	1950		1960		Stability	
	Interregional age structure	Intraregional age structure	Interregional age structure	Intraregional age structure	Interregional age structure	Intraregional age structure
California:						
0–9	0.0129	0.1839	0.0187	0.2129	0.0808	0.2775
10–19	0.0085	0.1212	0.0140	0.1600	0.0612	0.2102
20–29	0.0113	0.1604	0.0112	0.1273	0.0504	0.1731
30–39	0.0116	0.1653	0.0129	0.1475	0.0362	0.1244
40–49	0.0095	0.1358	0.0114	0.1301	0.0259	0.0889
50–59	0.0075	0.1063	0.0085	0.0972	0.0166	0.0570
60–69	0.0054	0.0774	0.0061	0.0701	0.0115	0.0396
70–79	0.0027	0.0382	0.0036	0.0417	0.0064	0.0220
80+	0.0008	0.0115	0.0012	0.0132	0.0021	0.0073
Subtotal	0.0702	1.0000	0.0876	1.0000	0.2911	1.0000
Regional decennial growth rate	—	1.5326	—	1.4847	—	1.2238
Rest of the U.S.:						
0–9	0.1819	0.1957	0.1989	0.2180	0.1471	0.2075
10–19	0.1357	0.1460	0.1532	0.1680	0.1301	0.1836
20–29	0.1462	0.1572	0.1097	0.1202	0.1088	0.1534
30–39	0.1394	0.1500	0.1233	0.1351	0.0979	0.1382
40–49	0.1184	0.1273	0.1140	0.1249	0.0814	0.1148
50–59	0.0954	0.1026	0.0921	0.1009	0.0631	0.0891
60–69	0.0680	0.0731	0.0686	0.0752	0.0448	0.0631
70–79	0.0343	0.0363	0.0412	0.0452	0.0268	0.0378
80+	0.0105	0.0113	0.0114	0.0125	0.0089	0.0125
Subtotal	0.9298	1.0000	0.9124	1.0000	0.7089	1.0000
Regional decennial growth rate	—	1.1230	—	1.1677	—	1.2238
Total	1.0000	—	1.0000	—	1.0000	—
National decennial growth rate	1.1445	—	1.1900	—	$\lambda = 1.2238$	—

[5] ——, "The Population Projection as a Matrix Operator," *Demography*, I (1964), 56–73.

[6] Leslie, P. H., "On the Use of Matrices in Certain Population Mathematics," *Biometrika*, XXXIII (November 1945), 183–212.

[7] ——, "Some Further Notes on the Use of Matrices in Population Mathematics," *Biometrika*, XXXV (December 1948), 213–245.

[8] Lopez, Alvaro, *Problems in Stable Population Theory* (Princeton, N.J.: Office of Population Research, Princeton University, 1961).

[9] Rogers, Andrei, "The Multiregional Matrix Growth Operator and the Stable Interregional Age Structure," *Demography*, III, 2 (1966), 537–544.

6 INTERVENTION

6.1. Introduction

In the absence of system intervention, the fundamental matrix growth model, $\mathbf{w}^{(t+1)} = G\mathbf{w}^{(t)}$, converges to a stable distribution. This distribution, however, may be incompatible with long-range planning goals. Thus intervention to effect a desired allocation of population to regions may be in order; an intervention, for example, which takes the form of a policy that seeks to attract a certain minimum number of people, each year, from one set of regions to another, thereby redirecting the interregional system toward the desired stable distribution.[1]

Two considerations immediately arise:

(1) Not all distributional goals are feasible given a particular regime of growth, G.

(2) If the goal is feasible, the right number of people must be transferred during each time period.

Let us define the number of people to be supplied or withdrawn from each region by a vector $\mathbf{f}$ which may have both positive and negative components. A positive f_i indicates the number of people which must be attracted into a region during each unit interval of time; a negative f_i denotes the population that has to be periodically withdrawn from region i. The vector $\mathbf{w}$, as before, describes a population distribution, G is the matrix growth operator, $\mathbf{v}$ is the stable interregional distribution in the absence of intervention, V is the matrix composed of identical stable column vectors $\mathbf{v}$, and $\mathbf{g}$ denotes the desired stable interregional distribution.

---

[1] This chapter borrows liberally from a model developed by John G. Kemeny and J. Laurie Snell in Chapter 6 of their book: *Mathematical Models in the Social Sciences* (Boston: Ginn and Co., 1962), pp. 66–77. The author wishes to acknowledge his debt to that seminal work.

It has been shown earlier that if **w** is the initial distribution of people over regions then $G\mathbf{w}$ is the distribution after one time period, $G\mathbf{w}^2$ after two, and $G^n\mathbf{w}$ after n time periods. We now introduce the effects of system intervention. The number of people transferred from region to region during the initial growth period changes the total in each region by $G^{n-1}\mathbf{f}$ after n periods. The addition of the vector **f** after the following iteration alters the total in each region by $G^{n-2}\mathbf{f}$ after n periods, and so on. Thus, the total population after n periods is

$$(6.1) \qquad G^n\mathbf{w} + \sum_{k=0}^{n-1} G^k\mathbf{f}.$$

Since the goal distribution is represented by **g**, clearly what is desired is that (6.1) should, in the limit, converge to the vector **g**. For such a goal to be feasible, however, we must include the restriction that during this limiting process the population of each region never becomes negative, i.e.,

$$(6.2) \qquad G^n\mathbf{w} + \sum_{k=0}^{n-1} G^k\mathbf{f} \geqq 0 \qquad \text{for all } k = 1, 2, \ldots, n-1.$$

At this point we need to identify three possible classes of growth regimes:

(1) a growth regime which maintains a constant, or "stationary," population, i.e., the dominant characteristic root $\lambda = 1$;

(2) a growth regime which generates a gradually declining population, i.e., the dominant characteristic root $\lambda < 1$; and, most commonly,

(3) a growth regime which develops a continually expanding population, i.e., the dominant characteristic root $\lambda > 1$.

6.2. The Stationary Population System

A stationary population system is an interregional population system whose every region has birth and death rates that are equal. Thus the total population of the interregional system remains constant over time. Hence the columns of the interregional growth operator, G, sum to unity. For such a system we may distinguish between two classes of intervention: (1) intervention with control over the migration flows between all regions,

Intervention

and (2) intervention with control over the migration flows between only a subset of regions.

Intervention with Full Control

Consider the second term in (6.1), i.e., the series $\mathbf{f} + G\mathbf{f} + G^2\mathbf{f} + \cdots$. For this series to converge, $G^k\mathbf{f}$ must tend to zero as k increases. But $G^k\mathbf{f}$ tends to $(\mathbf{1}'\mathbf{f})\mathbf{v}$, where $\mathbf{1}'$ is the unit row vector, and $\mathbf{v} \neq \mathbf{0}$. Hence a necessary condition for convergence is that $\mathbf{1}'\mathbf{f} = 0$. This means that to achieve a stable distribution the net total population transfer at each iteration must be zero. That is, the number of people attracted to regions in the system must equal the number which are removed from others. Hence we have

$$\mathbf{f} + G\mathbf{f} + G^2\mathbf{f} + \cdots = \mathbf{f} + \sum_{n=1}^{\infty} G^n\mathbf{f},$$

and since if $\mathbf{1}'\mathbf{f} = 0$, $V\mathbf{f} = \mathbf{0}$, we have a sufficient condition for convergence with

$$\mathbf{f} + \sum_{n=1}^{\infty} G^n\mathbf{f} = \mathbf{f} + \sum_{n=1}^{\infty} (G^n - V)\mathbf{f} = Z\mathbf{f}.$$

Thus to achieve the goal $\mathbf{g}$, we require

(6.3) $\qquad \mathbf{g} = (\mathbf{1}'\mathbf{w})\mathbf{v} + Z\mathbf{f}.$

Now noting that $G\mathbf{v} = \mathbf{v}$, $V\mathbf{v} = \mathbf{v}$, and $Z = (I - G + V)^{-1}$, we can solve (6.3) by multiplying through by Z^{-1} which yields

(6.4) $\qquad (I - G + V)\mathbf{g} = (\mathbf{1}'\mathbf{w})(\mathbf{v} - \mathbf{v} + \mathbf{v}) + \mathbf{f}.$

Since $\mathbf{1}'Z = \mathbf{1}'$, and because the net population transfer in each period is 0, the total population at any period must remain constant. Thus,

(6.5) $\qquad \mathbf{1}'\mathbf{g} = (\mathbf{1}'\mathbf{w})(\mathbf{1}'\mathbf{v}) + \mathbf{1}'\mathbf{f} = \mathbf{1}'\mathbf{w}.$

Let us now combine the results of (6.4) and (6.5) to derive

(6.6) $\qquad \mathbf{f} = (I - G)\mathbf{g}.$

To check that the total population transfer is still 0, note that $\mathbf{1}'G = \mathbf{1}'$ and $\mathbf{1}'(I - G) = \mathbf{0}'$, thus $\mathbf{1}'\mathbf{f} = 0$, and our requirement is satisfied.

In summary, we have shown that $\mathbf{1'g} = \mathbf{1'w}$ is the necessary and sufficient condition for the existence of an $\mathbf{f}$ such that

$$G^n\mathbf{w} + \sum_{k=0}^{n-1} G^k\mathbf{f}$$

converges to $\mathbf{g}$, in the limit, and we have established that the unique $\mathbf{f}$ which accomplishes this is given by

$$\mathbf{f} = (I - G)\mathbf{g}.$$

We must now check the nonnegativity constraint to establish feasibility. Replacing $\mathbf{f}$ by (6.6) in (6.2), we have

$$G^n\mathbf{w} + \sum_{k=0}^{n-1} G^k(I - G)\mathbf{g} \geqq 0,$$

and noting that $(I + G + G^2 + \cdots)(I - G) = (I - G^n)$ we reduce the constraint to

$$G^n\mathbf{w} + (I - G^n)\mathbf{g} \geqq 0,$$

or equivalently,

(6.7) $\qquad G^n(\mathbf{g} - \mathbf{w}) \leqq \mathbf{g}, \qquad$ for $n \geqq 0$.

This constraint may appear, at first, to be impossible to enforce since an infinite number of conditions are specified. However, a theorem by Kemeny and Snell provides an algorithm for establishing feasibility in a finite number of steps.[2]

The Kemeny-Snell Theorem

(i) If for some k the sum of the absolute values of the components of $G^k(\mathbf{g} - \mathbf{w})$ is no greater than the least entry of $\mathbf{g}$, then (6.7) holds for all $n \geqq k$; and this must occur for some k.

(ii) If $G^{k+1}(\mathbf{g} - \mathbf{w}) \leqq G^k(\mathbf{g} - \mathbf{w})$ and (6.7) holds for k, then (6.7) holds for $n \geqq k$.

(iii) If $G\mathbf{g} \leqq \mathbf{g}$, then (6.7) holds for all n, for all $\mathbf{w}$.

Proof. Let $\mathbf{h} = G^k(\mathbf{g} - \mathbf{w})$. Then $G^n(\mathbf{g} - \mathbf{w}) = G^{n-k}\mathbf{h}$, and the components of G to any power never exceed unity. Hence a component of $G^{n-k}\mathbf{h}$ is bounded by $\sum |h_i|$. Thus if

$$\sum_i |h_i| \leqq \min_i g_i,$$

---

[2] Kemeny and Snell, *op. cit.*, p. 68.

then (6.7) holds for $n \geq k$, and since $\mathbf{h} = G^k(\mathbf{g} - \mathbf{w})$ converges to $V\mathbf{g} - V\mathbf{w}$, which is zero by (6.3), $\mathbf{h}$ also tends to $\mathbf{0}$. Hence $\sum_i |h_i| \leq \min_i g_i$ for sufficiently high k. (Recall that the elements of $\mathbf{g}$ are by definition nonnegative.)

To establish (ii), note that if $G\mathbf{h} \leq \mathbf{h}$ then we can multiply both sides by the nonnegative matrix G^s to obtain $G^{s+1}\mathbf{h} \leq G^s\mathbf{h}$ and thereby show that $G^s\mathbf{h}$ is monotone decreasing.

Finally, if $G\mathbf{g} \leq \mathbf{g}$, then $G^{n+1}\mathbf{g} \leq \mathbf{g}$ for all n; hence (6.7) holds for all n, even without the term $G^n\mathbf{w}$. Thus (iii) holds.

With the Kemeny-Snell Theorem one has an effective procedure for checking (6.7) in a finite number of steps. That is, we compute $G^n(\mathbf{g} - \mathbf{w})$ for successive n, beginning with $n = 0$. If (6.7) is violated for any of these, then $\mathbf{g}$ is not feasible. Ultimately a vector satisfying condition (i) is reached, and if (6.7) has not been violated up to this point, it will never be violated and, therefore, $\mathbf{g}$ is feasible.

Parts (ii) and (iii) of the Theorem offer us shortcuts. Namely, if a computed vector does not exceed the previous one, one may stop. Alternatively, if $G\mathbf{g} \leq \mathbf{g}$, $\mathbf{g}$ is feasible and the entire computation is unnecessary.

Example.—To illustrate the stationary population model with full control let us turn to a three-region system (A, B, and C) with the following growth operator:

$$G = \begin{bmatrix} \frac{1}{3} & \frac{1}{4} & \frac{1}{3} \\ \frac{1}{3} & \frac{1}{2} & \frac{1}{3} \\ \frac{1}{3} & \frac{1}{4} & \frac{1}{3} \end{bmatrix}.$$

For this system, the stable distribution $\mathbf{v}' = (\frac{3}{10}, \frac{4}{10}, \frac{3}{10})$.[3] Thus, for example, an initial population distribution of $\mathbf{w}' = (16, 11, 9)$ will yield a stable distribution of $\mathbf{g}' = (10.8, 14.4, 10.8)$.

Assume that an equal distribution of population has been set as a goal for this three-region system. What are the required transfer levels? That is, what $\mathbf{f}$, added after each iteration, will provide, in the limit, a $\mathbf{g}' = (12, 12, 12)$?

---

[3] To conserve space we shall frequently denote column vectors in their transposed form.

$$\mathbf{f} = (I - G)\mathbf{g} = \begin{bmatrix} \frac{2}{3} & -\frac{1}{4} & -\frac{1}{3} \\ -\frac{1}{3} & \frac{1}{2} & -\frac{1}{3} \\ -\frac{1}{3} & -\frac{1}{4} & \frac{2}{3} \end{bmatrix} \begin{bmatrix} 12 \\ 12 \\ 12 \end{bmatrix} = \begin{bmatrix} 1 \\ -2 \\ 1 \end{bmatrix}$$

$$Z = (I - G + \mathbf{v}\mathbf{1}')^{-1} = \begin{bmatrix} .967 & .050 & -.033 \\ .067 & .900 & .067 \\ -.033 & .050 & .967 \end{bmatrix}^{-1}$$

$$= \begin{bmatrix} 1.04 & -.06 & .04 \\ -.08 & 1.12 & -.08 \\ .04 & -.06 & 1.04 \end{bmatrix}.$$

Checking condition (6.3):

$$\mathbf{g} = (\mathbf{1}'\mathbf{w})\mathbf{v} + Z\mathbf{f}$$

$$= 36 \begin{bmatrix} \frac{3}{10} \\ \frac{4}{10} \\ \frac{3}{10} \end{bmatrix} + \begin{bmatrix} 1.2 \\ -2.4 \\ 1.2 \end{bmatrix}$$

$$= \begin{bmatrix} 12 \\ 12 \\ 12 \end{bmatrix}.$$

Checking condition (6.7):

$$(\mathbf{g} - \mathbf{w}) = \begin{bmatrix} -4 \\ 1 \\ 3 \end{bmatrix}$$

$$\sum |h_i| = 8 < \min_i g_i.$$

Hence (6.7) is satisfied, and $\mathbf{g}' = (12, 12, 12)$ is feasible.

Intervention with Partial Control

Consider the problem of partial control. That is, suppose we can influence population transfers only in a subset of regions. Without loss of generality, we may assume that these regions are the first k of the m that constitute the system. This means that $\mathbf{f}_i = 0$ for $i > k$.

The results of the previous section are still applicable. However, we now must further restrict the set of feasible goals. The restriction will ensure that $\mathbf{f}$ has nonzero components only in regions $i = 1, \ldots, k$.

Intervention

Let us partition the matrix G into four submatrices:

$$G = \begin{array}{c} \\ \text{controlled} \\ \text{regions} \\ \text{uncontrolled} \\ \text{regions} \end{array} \overset{\begin{array}{cc}\text{controlled} & \text{uncontrolled}\end{array}}{\left[\begin{array}{c|c} T & Q \\ \hline U & W \end{array}\right]}.$$

Let $\mathbf{g} = \begin{bmatrix} \mathbf{g}^* \\ \mathbf{g}^{**} \end{bmatrix}$, with $\mathbf{g}^*$ containing the goals for the controlled regions.

(6.8) $\quad (I - G)\mathbf{g} = \begin{cases} \mathbf{g}^* - T\mathbf{g}^* - Q\mathbf{g}^{**} \text{ in controlled regions} \\ \mathbf{g}^{**} - U\mathbf{g}^* - W\mathbf{g}^{**} \text{ in all others.} \end{cases}$

Thus our new constraint is

$$\mathbf{g}^{**} - U\mathbf{g}^* - W\mathbf{g}^{**} = 0$$

or

$$(I - W)\mathbf{g}^{**} = U\mathbf{g}^*.$$

Since the columns of W sum to a number less than unity, $(I - W)$ has an inverse, and we have for our constraint

(6.9) $\quad\quad\quad\quad \mathbf{g}^{**} = (I - W)^{-1}U\mathbf{g}^*.$

Therefore, the policy-making body has no choice in values of $\mathbf{g}$ for the uncontrolled regions since once $\mathbf{g}^*$ is selected, $\mathbf{g}^{**}$ is strictly determined by (6.9). To compute the nonzero components of $\mathbf{f}$ from (6.9), we note that

$$\mathbf{f}^* = [I - T - Q(I - W)^{-1}U]\mathbf{g}^*,$$

and defining $G^* = T + Q(I - W)^{-1}U$, we have

(6.10) $\quad\quad\quad\quad \mathbf{f}^* = (I - G^*)\mathbf{g}^*.$

Notice that if $\mathbf{1}'G = \mathbf{1}'$, $\mathbf{1}'G^* = \mathbf{1}'$. Hence (6.10) guarantees that $\mathbf{1}'\mathbf{f}^* = 0$. Moreover, since $f_i = 0$ for uncontrolled regions $\mathbf{1}'\mathbf{f} = 0$. Thus for the stationary population model with incomplete control, $\mathbf{g}$ is feasible if, and only if, (6.5), (6.7), and (6.9) are satisfied, and in these instances (6.10) provides the solution.

Example.—Let us suppose that region C, in our example, is beyond the control of the policy-making body. Then, we have:

$$T = \begin{bmatrix} \frac{1}{3} & \frac{1}{4} \\ \frac{1}{3} & \frac{1}{2} \end{bmatrix} \qquad Q = \begin{bmatrix} \frac{1}{3} \\ \frac{1}{3} \end{bmatrix}$$

$$U = \begin{bmatrix} \frac{1}{3} & \frac{1}{4} \end{bmatrix} \qquad W = \begin{bmatrix} \frac{1}{3} \end{bmatrix}$$

$$(I - W)^{-1} = \frac{3}{2} \qquad Q(I - W)^{-1} = \begin{bmatrix} \frac{1}{2} \\ \frac{1}{2} \end{bmatrix}$$

$$G^* = \begin{bmatrix} \frac{1}{2} & \frac{3}{8} \\ \frac{1}{2} & \frac{5}{8} \end{bmatrix} \qquad Q(I - W)^{-1}U = \begin{bmatrix} \frac{1}{6} & \frac{1}{8} \\ \frac{1}{6} & \frac{1}{8} \end{bmatrix}.$$

If $\mathbf{w}' = (16, 11, 9)$, as before, then the restrictions on $g = (g_a, g_b, g_c)$ are

$$g_a + g_b + g_c = 36$$

and

$$g_c = \tfrac{1}{2}g_a + \tfrac{3}{8}g_b.$$

Or equivalently,

(6.11)
$$g_b = \tfrac{288}{11} - \tfrac{12}{11}g_a$$
$$g_c = \tfrac{108}{11} + \tfrac{1}{11}g_a.$$

To keep all elements of $\mathbf{g}$ greater than zero, one is restricted in selecting g_a by the inequality $0 < g_a < 24$. For any g_a within this range, g_b and g_c are determined by (6.11). The solution is

$$\mathbf{f}^* = (I - G^*)\mathbf{g}^*$$

or

$$f_a = \tfrac{1}{2}g_a - \tfrac{3}{8}g_b = \tfrac{10}{11}g_a - \tfrac{108}{11}$$

and

$$f_b = -f_a.$$

However, a further restriction in the choice of g_a is given by (6.7). Thus, for $g_a = 12$, we have

$$\mathbf{g}' = (12, 13.09, 10.91)$$

and

$$\mathbf{f}' = (1.09, -1.09, 0).$$

It is easily established that $\mathbf{g} = (\mathbf{1}'\mathbf{w})\mathbf{v} + Z\mathbf{f}$, as before, and that (6.7) is satisfied. Hence, $\mathbf{g}$ is feasible.

To clarify our discussion of system intervention in the stationary population model, we summarize the numerical results of this section in Tables 6.1 through 6.3.

Intervention

TABLE 6.1. THREE REGION EXAMPLE: NO INTERVENTION

$$\begin{bmatrix} 11.08 \\ 13.83 \\ 11.08 \end{bmatrix} = \begin{bmatrix} \frac{1}{3} & \frac{1}{4} & \frac{1}{3} \\ \frac{1}{3} & \frac{1}{2} & \frac{1}{3} \\ \frac{1}{3} & \frac{1}{4} & \frac{1}{3} \end{bmatrix} \begin{bmatrix} 16.00 \\ 11.00 \\ 9.00 \end{bmatrix}$$

$$\begin{bmatrix} 10.84 \\ 14.34 \\ 10.84 \end{bmatrix} = \begin{bmatrix} \frac{1}{3} & \frac{1}{4} & \frac{1}{3} \\ \frac{1}{3} & \frac{1}{2} & \frac{1}{3} \\ \frac{1}{3} & \frac{1}{4} & \frac{1}{3} \end{bmatrix} \begin{bmatrix} 11.08 \\ 13.83 \\ 11.08 \end{bmatrix}$$

$$\begin{bmatrix} 10.80 \\ 14.39 \\ 10.80 \end{bmatrix} = \begin{bmatrix} \frac{1}{3} & \frac{1}{4} & \frac{1}{3} \\ \frac{1}{3} & \frac{1}{2} & \frac{1}{3} \\ \frac{1}{3} & \frac{1}{4} & \frac{1}{3} \end{bmatrix} \begin{bmatrix} 10.84 \\ 14.34 \\ 10.84 \end{bmatrix}$$

$$\begin{bmatrix} 10.80 \\ 14.40 \\ 10.80 \end{bmatrix} = \begin{bmatrix} \frac{1}{3} & \frac{1}{4} & \frac{1}{3} \\ \frac{1}{3} & \frac{1}{2} & \frac{1}{3} \\ \frac{1}{3} & \frac{1}{4} & \frac{1}{3} \end{bmatrix} \begin{bmatrix} 10.80 \\ 14.39 \\ 10.80 \end{bmatrix}$$

6.3. Interregional Distributional Goals and System Intervention in California: The Stationary Population Model

The application of the stationary intervention model to interregional flows in California is relatively straightforward. For ease of exposition let us focus on the four-region growth operator presented in Table 6.4. Here the state has been divided into three regions: the San Francisco–Oakland SMSA, the Los

TABLE 6.2. THREE REGION EXAMPLE: INTERVENTION WITH FULL CONTROL

$$\begin{bmatrix} 12.08 \\ 11.83 \\ 12.08 \end{bmatrix} = \begin{bmatrix} \frac{1}{3} & \frac{1}{4} & \frac{1}{3} \\ \frac{1}{3} & \frac{1}{2} & \frac{1}{3} \\ \frac{1}{3} & \frac{1}{4} & \frac{1}{3} \end{bmatrix} \begin{bmatrix} 16.00 \\ 11.00 \\ 9.00 \end{bmatrix} + \begin{bmatrix} 1 \\ -2 \\ 1 \end{bmatrix} = \begin{bmatrix} 11.08 \\ 13.83 \\ 11.08 \end{bmatrix} + \begin{bmatrix} 1 \\ -2 \\ 1 \end{bmatrix}$$

$$\begin{bmatrix} 12.02 \\ 11.97 \\ 12.02 \end{bmatrix} = \begin{bmatrix} \frac{1}{3} & \frac{1}{4} & \frac{1}{3} \\ \frac{1}{3} & \frac{1}{2} & \frac{1}{3} \\ \frac{1}{3} & \frac{1}{4} & \frac{1}{3} \end{bmatrix} \begin{bmatrix} 12.08 \\ 11.83 \\ 12.08 \end{bmatrix} + \begin{bmatrix} 1 \\ -2 \\ 1 \end{bmatrix} = \begin{bmatrix} 11.02 \\ 13.97 \\ 11.02 \end{bmatrix} + \begin{bmatrix} 1 \\ -2 \\ 1 \end{bmatrix}$$

$$\begin{bmatrix} 12.00 \\ 12.00 \\ 12.00 \end{bmatrix} = \begin{bmatrix} \frac{1}{3} & \frac{1}{4} & \frac{1}{3} \\ \frac{1}{3} & \frac{1}{2} & \frac{1}{3} \\ \frac{1}{3} & \frac{1}{4} & \frac{1}{3} \end{bmatrix} \begin{bmatrix} 12.02 \\ 11.97 \\ 12.02 \end{bmatrix} + \begin{bmatrix} 1 \\ -2 \\ 1 \end{bmatrix} = \begin{bmatrix} 11.00 \\ 14.00 \\ 11.00 \end{bmatrix} + \begin{bmatrix} 1 \\ -2 \\ 1 \end{bmatrix}$$

$$\begin{bmatrix} 12.00 \\ 12.00 \\ 12.00 \end{bmatrix} = \begin{bmatrix} \frac{1}{3} & \frac{1}{4} & \frac{1}{3} \\ \frac{1}{3} & \frac{1}{2} & \frac{1}{3} \\ \frac{1}{3} & \frac{1}{4} & \frac{1}{3} \end{bmatrix} \begin{bmatrix} 12.00 \\ 12.00 \\ 12.00 \end{bmatrix} + \begin{bmatrix} 1 \\ -2 \\ 1 \end{bmatrix} = \begin{bmatrix} 11.00 \\ 14.00 \\ 11.00 \end{bmatrix} + \begin{bmatrix} 1 \\ -2 \\ 1 \end{bmatrix}$$

TABLE 6.3. Three Region Example: Intervention
with Partial Control

$$\begin{bmatrix} 12.17 \\ 12.74 \\ 11.08 \end{bmatrix} = \begin{bmatrix} \frac{1}{3} & \frac{1}{4} & \frac{1}{3} \\ \frac{1}{3} & \frac{1}{2} & \frac{1}{3} \\ \frac{1}{3} & \frac{1}{4} & \frac{1}{3} \end{bmatrix} \begin{bmatrix} 16.00 \\ 11.00 \\ 9.00 \end{bmatrix} + \begin{bmatrix} 1.09 \\ -1.09 \\ 0 \end{bmatrix} = \begin{bmatrix} 11.08 \\ 13.83 \\ 11.08 \end{bmatrix} + \begin{bmatrix} 1.09 \\ -1.09 \\ 0 \end{bmatrix}$$

$$\begin{bmatrix} 12.03 \\ 13.03 \\ 10.94 \end{bmatrix} = \begin{bmatrix} \frac{1}{3} & \frac{1}{4} & \frac{1}{3} \\ \frac{1}{3} & \frac{1}{2} & \frac{1}{3} \\ \frac{1}{3} & \frac{1}{4} & \frac{1}{3} \end{bmatrix} \begin{bmatrix} 12.17 \\ 12.74 \\ 11.08 \end{bmatrix} + \begin{bmatrix} 1.09 \\ -1.09 \\ 0 \end{bmatrix} = \begin{bmatrix} 10.94 \\ 14.12 \\ 10.94 \end{bmatrix} + \begin{bmatrix} 1.09 \\ -1.09 \\ 0 \end{bmatrix}$$

$$\begin{bmatrix} 12.00 \\ 13.09 \\ 10.91 \end{bmatrix} = \begin{bmatrix} \frac{1}{3} & \frac{1}{4} & \frac{1}{3} \\ \frac{1}{3} & \frac{1}{2} & \frac{1}{3} \\ \frac{1}{3} & \frac{1}{4} & \frac{1}{3} \end{bmatrix} \begin{bmatrix} 12.03 \\ 13.03 \\ 10.94 \end{bmatrix} + \begin{bmatrix} 1.09 \\ -1.09 \\ 0 \end{bmatrix} = \begin{bmatrix} 11.91 \\ 14.18 \\ 10.91 \end{bmatrix} + \begin{bmatrix} 1.09 \\ -1.09 \\ 0 \end{bmatrix}$$

$$\begin{bmatrix} 12.00 \\ 13.09 \\ 10.91 \end{bmatrix} = \begin{bmatrix} \frac{1}{3} & \frac{1}{4} & \frac{1}{3} \\ \frac{1}{3} & \frac{1}{2} & \frac{1}{3} \\ \frac{1}{3} & \frac{1}{4} & \frac{1}{3} \end{bmatrix} \begin{bmatrix} 12.00 \\ 13.09 \\ 10.91 \end{bmatrix} + \begin{bmatrix} 1.09 \\ -1.09 \\ 0 \end{bmatrix} = \begin{bmatrix} 11.91 \\ 14.18 \\ 10.91 \end{bmatrix} + \begin{bmatrix} 1.09 \\ -1.09 \\ 0 \end{bmatrix}$$

Angeles–Long Beach SMSA, and the rest of the state. The rest of the U.S. completes the interregional system. Let us assume a partial control situation with control available only over movement into and out of the three California regions.

TABLE 6.4. Growth Operator, Stable Distribution, and the 1955 Population Distribution for California Regions and the Rest of the United States: The Stationary Population Model

Growth operator:

$$G = \begin{bmatrix} .8544 & .0076 & .0219 & .0017 \\ .0172 & .8907 & .0306 & .0056 \\ .0688 & .0475 & .8737 & .0054 \\ .0596 & .0542 & .0738 & .9873 \end{bmatrix}$$

Stable distribution:*

$$\begin{array}{cccc} & A & F & CAL. & U.S. \\ \mathbf{v'} = (& .0244 & .0674 & .0743 & .8339) \end{array}$$

1955 Population distribution:

$$\begin{array}{cccc} & A & F & CAL. & U.S. \\ \mathbf{w'} = (& 2{,}547{,}000 & 5{,}332{,}000 & 5{,}109{,}000 & 152{,}082{,}000) \\ & (.0154) & (.0323) & (.0310) & (.9213) \end{array}$$

* A = San Francisco–Oakland SMSA; F = Los Angeles–Long Beach SMSA; $CAL.$ = Rest of California; $U.S.$ = Rest of the United States.

Intervention

Consider the stable distribution in the absence of intervention. This distribution suggests that the four-region system is heading toward a long-run distribution with 2.44 percent of the national population residing in the San Francisco–Oakland SMSA, 6.74 percent in the Los Angeles–Long Beach SMSA, 7.43 percent in the rest of California, and 83.39 percent in the rest of the United States. Assume that we wish to limit the expected stable populations of the two SMSA's to 3 and 6 percent of the national total, respectively. Is such a goal feasible? What transfer levels are required to direct the system toward this desired stable distribution?

Proceeding according to the steps outlined in the last section, we first find:

$$T = \begin{bmatrix} .8544 & .0076 & .0219 \\ .0172 & .8907 & .0306 \\ .0688 & .0475 & .8737 \end{bmatrix} \quad Q = \begin{bmatrix} .0017 \\ .0056 \\ .0054 \end{bmatrix}$$

$$U = [.0596 \quad .0542 \quad .0738] \quad W = [.9873]$$

$$G^* = \begin{bmatrix} .8624 & .0149 & .0318 \\ .0435 & .9146 & .0631 \\ .0941 & .0706 & .9051 \end{bmatrix}.$$

Now recalling that we lose one degree of freedom in the selection of goals because of the constraint $\mathbf{1'g} = \mathbf{1'w}$, we derive our "goal" for the third region, i.e., the rest of California:

$$g_A + g_F + g_{Cal} + g_{US} = 165{,}070{,}000$$

$$4.6929 g_A + 4.2677 g_F + 5.8110 g_{Cal} - g_{US} = 0$$

where

$$g_A = .03(165{,}070{,}000) = 4{,}952{,}000 = 5{,}000{,}000$$

and

$$g_F = .06(165{,}070{,}000) = 9{,}904{,}000 = 10{,}000{,}000.$$

Solving the two equations in two unknowns we find g_{Cal} and hence our full set of goals is

$$\mathbf{g}^* = \begin{bmatrix} 5{,}000{,}000 \\ 10{,}000{,}000 \\ 12{,}320{,}000 \end{bmatrix}.$$

Recall that once **g*** is specified, **g*** * is strictly determined by the relation [Equation (6.9)]:

$$\mathbf{g}^{**} = (I - W)^{-1}U\mathbf{g}^*.$$

Thus, the population of the noncontrollable region, i.e., the rest of the U.S., which follows from our choice of **g*** is

$$g_{US} = 137{,}750{,}000.$$

After first establishing the feasibility of our choice of **g*** by means of the Kemeny-Snell Theorem, we calculate the intervention vector **f**:

$$\mathbf{f}^* = (I - G^*)\mathbf{g}^*$$

$$= \begin{bmatrix} 148{,}000 \\ -141{,}500 \\ -6{,}500 \end{bmatrix}.$$

This computation indicates that to redirect the system away from a stable distribution of (.0244/.0674/.0743/.8339) toward one of (.0300/.0600/.0750/.8350) we must, during each interval of time, transfer 141,500 people from the Los Angeles–Long Beach SMSA and 6,500 from the rest of California region to the San Francisco–Oakland SMSA. Table 6.5 illustrates the convergence. Table 6.6 presents alternative goal distributions and their associated intervention vectors.

6.4. The Declining Population System

A declining population system is an interregional population system whose total population declines over time as a result of an excess of deaths over births. Hence at least one of the columns of the interregional growth operator, G, sums to a number less than unity. As in the stationary population model, we may distinguish between two classes of intervention: (1) intervention with full control, and (2) intervention with partial control. However, unlike the stationary model, we no longer can assume that the number of people attracted to regions in the system must equal the number which are removed from others. Such an assumption would result in the ultimate extinction of the interregional population. For nontrivial results, therefore, we make the assumption that people are injected into the interregional system, at each time period, in sufficient amounts to compensate

TABLE 6.5. STATIONARY POPULATION MODEL FOR CALIFORNIA: PARTIAL CONTROL*

$$\begin{matrix}A\\F\\CAL.\\U.S.\end{matrix}\begin{bmatrix}2{,}735\\5{,}659.5\\5{,}707\\150{,}968\end{bmatrix}=\begin{bmatrix}.8544&.0076&.0219&.0017\\.0172&.8907&.0306&.0056\\.0688&.0475&.8737&.0054\\.0596&.0542&.0733&.9873\end{bmatrix}\begin{bmatrix}2{,}547\\5{,}332\\5{,}109\\152{,}082\end{bmatrix}+\begin{bmatrix}148\\-141.5\\-6.5\\0\end{bmatrix}=\begin{bmatrix}2{,}587\\5{,}801\\5{,}713.5\\150{,}968\end{bmatrix}+\begin{bmatrix}148\\-141.5\\-6.5\\0\end{bmatrix}$$

$$\begin{matrix}A\\F\\CAL.\\U.S.\end{matrix}\begin{bmatrix}2{,}909\\5{,}966.5\\6{,}252\\149{,}942\end{bmatrix}=\begin{bmatrix}.8544&.0076&.0219&.0017\\.0172&.8907&.0306&.0056\\.0688&.0475&.8727&.0054\\.0596&.0542&.0738&.9873\end{bmatrix}\begin{bmatrix}2{,}735\\5{,}659.5\\5{,}707\\150{,}968\end{bmatrix}+\begin{bmatrix}148\\-141.5\\-6.5\\0\end{bmatrix}=\begin{bmatrix}2{,}761\\6{,}108\\6{,}258.5\\149{,}942\end{bmatrix}+\begin{bmatrix}148\\-141.5\\-6.5\\0\end{bmatrix}$$

$$\vdots$$

$$\begin{matrix}A\\F\\CAL.\\U.S.\end{matrix}\begin{bmatrix}5{,}000\\10{,}000\\12{,}320\\137{,}750\end{bmatrix}**=\begin{bmatrix}.8544&.0076&.0219&.0017\\.0172&.8907&.0306&.0056\\.0688&.0475&.8737&.0054\\.0596&.0542&.0738&.9873\end{bmatrix}\begin{bmatrix}5{,}000\\10{,}000\\12{,}320\\137{,}750\end{bmatrix}+\begin{bmatrix}148\\-141.5\\-6.5\\0\end{bmatrix}=\begin{bmatrix}4{,}852\\10{,}141.5\\12{,}326.5\\137{,}750\end{bmatrix}+\begin{bmatrix}148\\-141.5\\-6.5\\0\end{bmatrix}$$

* Population figures are in thousands.
** Errors due to rounding preclude the strict convergence shown in this table.

TABLE 6.6. Alternative Distributional Goals for California Regions and Their Policy Implications: The Stationary Population Model with Partial Control

$$\mathbf{v'} = \begin{matrix} A & F & CAL. & U.S. \\ (4.028; & 11{,}126; & 12{,}265; & 137{,}652) \\ (.0244; & .0674; & .0743; & .8339) \end{matrix}$$

Stable Distribution (in 000's)

Goal Distribution (in 000's) $\mathbf{g'}$				Intervention Vector (in 000's) $\mathbf{f'}$			
A	F	CAL.	U.S.	A	F	CAL.	U.S.
1. (5,000;	10,000;	12,320;	137,750)	(148;	−141.5;	−6.5;	0)
$\mathbf{v'}$ = (.0303;	.0606;	.0746;	.8345)				
2. (6,000;	9.000;	12,260;	137,810)	(302;	−266 ;	−36 ;	0)
$\mathbf{v'}$ = (.0363;	.0545;	.0743;	.8349)				
3. (4,000;	12,000;	11,612;	137,458)	(3;	118 ;	−121 ;	0)
$\mathbf{v'}$ = (.0242;	.0727;	.0703;	.8328)				
4. (8,000;	8,000;	11,362;	137,708)	(621;	−382 ;	−239 ;	0)
$\mathbf{v'}$ = (.0485;	.0485;	.0688;	.8342)				
5. (3,000;	9,000;	14,768;	137,302)	(−190;	−294 ;	484 ;	0)
$\mathbf{v'}$ = (.0182;	.0545;	.0895;	.8318)				

for the negative rate of natural increase. More specifically, we assume that $\mathbf{1'f} > s$ where s is a sufficiently large positive integer to prevent the extinction of the population.

Intervention with Full Control

The mathematical analysis of the declining population model is almost identical to that of the stationary population model. For a declining population, G^n tends to zero as n increases; therefore, the first term of (6.1) tends to $\mathbf{0}$. Thus, to achieve a desired goal, $\sum_{k=0}^{n-1} G^k \mathbf{f}$ must tend to $\mathbf{g}$ as $n \to \infty$.

Since

$$I + G + G^2 + \cdots = (I - G)^{-1},$$

we have

(6.12) $$\mathbf{f} = (I - G)\mathbf{g}.$$

Intervention

If **g** is feasible, the unique **f** given by (6.12) will achieve the goal. The nonnegativity constraint becomes

$$G^n\mathbf{w} + \sum_{k=0}^{n-1} G^k(I - G)\mathbf{g} = G^n\mathbf{w} + (I - G^n)\mathbf{g} \geq 0$$

or

(6.13) $\qquad G^n(\mathbf{g} - \mathbf{w}) \leq \mathbf{g} \qquad$ for $n \geq 0$.

As in the stationary population model, the Kemeny-Snell Theorem provides an algorithm for establishing whether a particular **g** is feasible. The Theorem and the proof for the case of the declining population model are almost identical with those for the stationary model. One only needs to recall that **h** tends to **0** since $G^k \to 0$ as n increases and thus $\mathbf{h} = G^k(\mathbf{g} - \mathbf{w})$ also converges to **0**.

Example.—To illustrate the declining population model with full control let us analyze intervention in our three-region system (A, B, and C) with the following growth operator:

$$G = \begin{matrix} & \begin{matrix} A & B & C \end{matrix} \\ \begin{matrix} A \\ B \\ C \end{matrix} & \begin{bmatrix} \frac{1}{4} & \frac{1}{5} & \frac{1}{4} \\ \frac{1}{4} & \frac{2}{5} & \frac{1}{4} \\ \frac{1}{4} & \frac{1}{5} & \frac{1}{4} \end{bmatrix} \end{matrix}$$

and

$$(I - G)^{-1} = \begin{bmatrix} 2.00 & 1.00 & 1.00 \\ 1.25 & 2.50 & 1.25 \\ 1.00 & 1.00 & 2.00 \end{bmatrix}.$$

Thus, if $\mathbf{g}' = (12, 12, 12)$, then $\mathbf{f} = (\mathbf{g} - G\mathbf{g}) = (3.6, 1.2, 3.6)'$. We verify that $(I - G)^{-1}\mathbf{f} = \mathbf{g}$, and since $G\mathbf{g} \leq \mathbf{g}$, condition (iii) of the Kemeny-Snell Theorem is satisfied. Hence, **g** is feasible.

Intervention with Partial Control

In the declining population model, G^* is formed in an analogous manner to the G^* in the stationary model. The only difference is that the column sums no longer sum to unity. For the declining population model, **g** is feasible if, and only if, (6.9) and (6.13) hold, and in such instances the unique solution is

(6.14) $\qquad \mathbf{f}^* = (I - G^*)\mathbf{g}^*.$

Example.—Let us reconsider the three-region declining example presented above, and once again suppose that we have no control over region C.

$$T = \begin{bmatrix} \frac{1}{4} & \frac{1}{5} \\ \frac{1}{4} & \frac{2}{5} \end{bmatrix} \qquad Q = \begin{bmatrix} \frac{1}{4} \\ \frac{1}{4} \end{bmatrix}$$

$$U = \begin{bmatrix} \frac{1}{4} & \frac{1}{5} \end{bmatrix} \qquad W = \begin{bmatrix} \frac{1}{4} \end{bmatrix}$$

$$(I - W)^{-1} = \frac{4}{3} \qquad Q(I - W)^{-1} = \begin{bmatrix} \frac{1}{3} \\ \frac{1}{3} \end{bmatrix} \qquad G^* = \begin{bmatrix} \frac{1}{3} & \frac{4}{15} \\ \frac{1}{3} & \frac{7}{15} \end{bmatrix}.$$

Our restrictions over **g** now require

$$g_c = \tfrac{1}{3} g_a + \tfrac{4}{15} g_b.$$

Since $f_c = 0$ and $\mathbf{f}^* = (I - G^*)\mathbf{g}^*$, we have

$$f_a = \tfrac{2}{3} g_a - \tfrac{4}{15} g_b; \qquad f_b = \tfrac{8}{15} g_b - \tfrac{1}{3} g_a.$$

Thus, for example, with a $\mathbf{g}' = (12, 12, 7.2)$ we have

$$\mathbf{f} = \begin{bmatrix} 4.8 \\ 2.4 \\ 0 \end{bmatrix}.$$

To clarify the above discussion of the declining population model, we once again summarize the numerical results in tabular form (Tables 6.7, 6.8, and 6.9).

TABLE 6.7. Three Region Example: No Intervention

$$\begin{bmatrix} 8.45 \\ 10.65 \\ 8.45 \end{bmatrix} = \begin{bmatrix} \frac{1}{4} & \frac{1}{5} & \frac{1}{4} \\ \frac{1}{4} & \frac{2}{5} & \frac{1}{4} \\ \frac{1}{4} & \frac{1}{5} & \frac{1}{4} \end{bmatrix} \begin{bmatrix} 16.00 \\ 11.00 \\ 9.00 \end{bmatrix}$$

$$\begin{bmatrix} 6.36 \\ 8.46 \\ 6.36 \end{bmatrix} = \begin{bmatrix} \frac{1}{4} & \frac{1}{5} & \frac{1}{4} \\ \frac{1}{4} & \frac{2}{5} & \frac{1}{4} \\ \frac{1}{4} & \frac{1}{5} & \frac{1}{4} \end{bmatrix} \begin{bmatrix} 8.45 \\ 10.65 \\ 8.45 \end{bmatrix}$$

$$\begin{bmatrix} 4.87 \\ 6.56 \\ 4.87 \end{bmatrix} = \begin{bmatrix} \frac{1}{4} & \frac{1}{5} & \frac{1}{4} \\ \frac{1}{4} & \frac{2}{5} & \frac{1}{4} \\ \frac{1}{4} & \frac{1}{5} & \frac{1}{4} \end{bmatrix} \begin{bmatrix} 6.36 \\ 8.46 \\ 6.36 \end{bmatrix}$$

$$\vdots$$

$$\begin{bmatrix} 0.00 \\ 0.00 \\ 0.00 \end{bmatrix} = \begin{bmatrix} \frac{1}{4} & \frac{1}{5} & \frac{1}{4} \\ \frac{1}{4} & \frac{2}{5} & \frac{1}{4} \\ \frac{1}{4} & \frac{1}{5} & \frac{1}{4} \end{bmatrix} \begin{bmatrix} 0.00 \\ 0.00 \\ 0.00 \end{bmatrix}$$

Intervention

TABLE 6.8. THREE REGION EXAMPLE: INTERVENTION WITH FULL CONTROL

$$\begin{bmatrix}12.05\\11.85\\12.05\end{bmatrix}=\begin{bmatrix}\frac{1}{4}&\frac{1}{5}&\frac{1}{4}\\\frac{1}{4}&\frac{2}{5}&\frac{1}{4}\\\frac{1}{4}&\frac{1}{5}&\frac{1}{4}\end{bmatrix}\begin{bmatrix}16.00\\11.00\\9.00\end{bmatrix}+\begin{bmatrix}3.6\\1.2\\3.6\end{bmatrix}=\begin{bmatrix}8.45\\10.65\\8.45\end{bmatrix}+\begin{bmatrix}3.6\\1.2\\3.6\end{bmatrix}$$

$$\begin{bmatrix}11.99\\11.96\\11.99\end{bmatrix}=\begin{bmatrix}\frac{1}{4}&\frac{1}{5}&\frac{1}{4}\\\frac{1}{4}&\frac{2}{5}&\frac{1}{4}\\\frac{1}{4}&\frac{1}{5}&\frac{1}{4}\end{bmatrix}\begin{bmatrix}12.05\\11.85\\12.05\end{bmatrix}+\begin{bmatrix}3.6\\1.2\\3.6\end{bmatrix}=\begin{bmatrix}8.39\\10.76\\8.39\end{bmatrix}+\begin{bmatrix}3.6\\1.2\\3.6\end{bmatrix}$$

$$\begin{bmatrix}11.99\\11.98\\11.99\end{bmatrix}=\begin{bmatrix}\frac{1}{4}&\frac{1}{5}&\frac{1}{4}\\\frac{1}{4}&\frac{2}{5}&\frac{1}{4}\\\frac{1}{4}&\frac{1}{5}&\frac{1}{4}\end{bmatrix}\begin{bmatrix}11.99\\11.96\\11.99\end{bmatrix}+\begin{bmatrix}3.6\\1.2\\3.6\end{bmatrix}=\begin{bmatrix}8.39\\10.78\\8.39\end{bmatrix}+\begin{bmatrix}3.6\\1.2\\3.6\end{bmatrix}$$

$$\vdots$$

$$\begin{bmatrix}12.00\\12.00\\12.00\end{bmatrix}=\begin{bmatrix}\frac{1}{4}&\frac{1}{5}&\frac{1}{4}\\\frac{1}{4}&\frac{2}{5}&\frac{1}{4}\\\frac{1}{4}&\frac{1}{5}&\frac{1}{4}\end{bmatrix}\begin{bmatrix}12.00\\12.00\\12.00\end{bmatrix}+\begin{bmatrix}3.6\\1.2\\3.6\end{bmatrix}=\begin{bmatrix}8.40\\10.80\\8.40\end{bmatrix}+\begin{bmatrix}3.6\\1.2\\3.6\end{bmatrix}$$

TABLE 6.9. THREE REGION EXAMPLE: INTERVENTION WITH PARTIAL CONTROL

$$\begin{bmatrix}13.25\\13.05\\8.45\end{bmatrix}=\begin{bmatrix}\frac{1}{4}&\frac{1}{5}&\frac{1}{4}\\\frac{1}{4}&\frac{2}{5}&\frac{1}{4}\\\frac{1}{4}&\frac{1}{5}&\frac{1}{4}\end{bmatrix}\begin{bmatrix}16.00\\11.00\\9.00\end{bmatrix}+\begin{bmatrix}4.8\\2.4\\0\end{bmatrix}=\begin{bmatrix}8.45\\10.65\\8.45\end{bmatrix}+\begin{bmatrix}4.8\\2.4\\0\end{bmatrix}$$

$$\begin{bmatrix}12.84\\13.05\\8.04\end{bmatrix}=\begin{bmatrix}\frac{1}{4}&\frac{1}{5}&\frac{1}{4}\\\frac{1}{4}&\frac{2}{5}&\frac{1}{4}\\\frac{1}{4}&\frac{1}{5}&\frac{1}{4}\end{bmatrix}\begin{bmatrix}13.25\\13.05\\8.45\end{bmatrix}+\begin{bmatrix}4.8\\2.4\\0\end{bmatrix}=\begin{bmatrix}8.04\\10.65\\8.04\end{bmatrix}+\begin{bmatrix}4.8\\2.4\\0\end{bmatrix}$$

$$\begin{bmatrix}12.64\\12.85\\7.84\end{bmatrix}=\begin{bmatrix}\frac{1}{4}&\frac{1}{5}&\frac{1}{4}\\\frac{1}{4}&\frac{2}{5}&\frac{1}{4}\\\frac{1}{4}&\frac{1}{5}&\frac{1}{4}\end{bmatrix}\begin{bmatrix}12.84\\13.05\\8.04\end{bmatrix}+\begin{bmatrix}4.8\\2.4\\0\end{bmatrix}=\begin{bmatrix}7.84\\10.45\\7.84\end{bmatrix}+\begin{bmatrix}4.8\\2.4\\0\end{bmatrix}$$

$$\vdots$$

$$\begin{bmatrix}12.00\\12.00\\7.20\end{bmatrix}=\begin{bmatrix}\frac{1}{4}&\frac{1}{5}&\frac{1}{4}\\\frac{1}{4}&\frac{2}{5}&\frac{1}{4}\\\frac{1}{4}&\frac{1}{5}&\frac{1}{4}\end{bmatrix}\begin{bmatrix}12.00\\12.00\\7.20\end{bmatrix}+\begin{bmatrix}4.8\\2.4\\0\end{bmatrix}=\begin{bmatrix}7.20\\9.60\\7.20\end{bmatrix}+\begin{bmatrix}4.8\\2.4\\0\end{bmatrix}$$

6.5. The Expanding Population System

An expanding population system is an interregional population system whose total population increases over time as a result of an excess of births over deaths. This is the most commonly observed population system. Unfortunately it is also the most intractable one to analyze within our framework. No analytic solution is immediately apparent. However, the following heuristic argument seems plausible and has led to successful results in a sample of numerical trials.

We begin by recalling the fundamental equation that defines the effects of intervention after n periods [Equation (6.1)]:

$$G^n \mathbf{w} + \sum_{k=0}^{n-1} G^k \mathbf{f}.$$

Recall also that an interregional population, $\mathbf{w}$, exposed to an unchanging regime of growth, G, will ultimately grow at an intrinsic rate of growth, λ, which is equal to the dominant characteristic root of the growth matrix, G. It would appear, then, that a generalization of (6.1) might be:

$$(6.15) \qquad G^n \mathbf{w} + \sum_{k=0}^{n-1} G^k \lambda^{k+1} \mathbf{f}.$$

Equation (6.14) suggests the following solution method for the expanding population model:

(1) Transform the expanding population growth operator, G, into its stationary population counterpart by reducing each diagonal element until the elements of each column in the operator sum to unity.

(2) Find the intervention vector, $\mathbf{f}$, for this stationary "counterpart" model.

(3) Increase the intervention vector, $\mathbf{f}$, by the intrinsic rate of growth, λ, at each iteration. (Thus at stability both the population and the intervention vector grow at the same intrinsic rate of growth, λ.)

Example.—To illustrate the above solution method let us once again return to our three-region example (A, B, and C) and assume the following expanding growth operator:

Intervention

$$G = \begin{bmatrix} \frac{1}{2} & \frac{1}{4} & \frac{1}{3} \\ \frac{1}{3} & \frac{3}{4} & \frac{1}{3} \\ \frac{1}{3} & \frac{1}{4} & \frac{1}{2} \end{bmatrix}.$$

For this system, the intrinsic rate of growth $\lambda = 1.2$ and the stable distribution $\mathbf{v}' = (.3, .4, .3)$. Assume that an equal distribution has been set as a goal for this three-region system. What are the required transfer levels after each iteration?

We begin by solving the stationary "counterpart" model. This was done in our earlier discussion of the stationary population model. There we found that the necessary intervention vector was:

$$\mathbf{f} = \begin{bmatrix} 1 \\ -2 \\ 1 \end{bmatrix}.$$

Hence our solution is to intervene with $\lambda \mathbf{f} = (1.2) \begin{bmatrix} 1 \\ -2 \\ 1 \end{bmatrix}$ after the first iteration, with $\lambda^2 \mathbf{f} = (1.2)^2 \begin{bmatrix} 1 \\ -2 \\ 1 \end{bmatrix}$ after the second, and so on. Table 6.10 illustrates the convergence to the goal of an equal distribution of population over the three regions.

TABLE 6.10. THREE REGION EXAMPLE: INTERVENTION
WITH FULL CONTROL

$$\begin{bmatrix} 14.9 \\ 14.2 \\ 13.8 \end{bmatrix} = \begin{bmatrix} \frac{1}{2} & \frac{1}{4} & \frac{1}{3} \\ \frac{1}{3} & \frac{3}{4} & \frac{1}{3} \\ \frac{1}{3} & \frac{1}{4} & \frac{1}{2} \end{bmatrix} \begin{bmatrix} 16.0 \\ 11.0 \\ 9.0 \end{bmatrix} + (1.2) \begin{bmatrix} 1 \\ -2 \\ 1 \end{bmatrix} = \begin{bmatrix} 13.7 \\ 16.6 \\ 12.6 \end{bmatrix} + \begin{bmatrix} 1.2 \\ -2.4 \\ 1.2 \end{bmatrix}$$

$$\begin{bmatrix} 17.1 \\ 17.3 \\ 16.7 \end{bmatrix} = \begin{bmatrix} \frac{1}{2} & \frac{1}{4} & \frac{1}{3} \\ \frac{1}{3} & \frac{3}{4} & \frac{1}{3} \\ \frac{1}{3} & \frac{1}{4} & \frac{1}{2} \end{bmatrix} \begin{bmatrix} 14.9 \\ 14.2 \\ 13.8 \end{bmatrix} + (1.2)^2 \begin{bmatrix} 1 \\ -2 \\ 1 \end{bmatrix} = \begin{bmatrix} 15.7 \\ 20.2 \\ 15.3 \end{bmatrix} + \begin{bmatrix} 1.4 \\ -2.9 \\ 1.4 \end{bmatrix}$$

$$\begin{bmatrix} 20.2 \\ 20.8 \\ 20.2 \end{bmatrix} = \begin{bmatrix} \frac{1}{2} & \frac{1}{4} & \frac{1}{3} \\ \frac{1}{3} & \frac{3}{4} & \frac{1}{3} \\ \frac{1}{3} & \frac{1}{4} & \frac{1}{2} \end{bmatrix} \begin{bmatrix} 17.1 \\ 17.3 \\ 16.7 \end{bmatrix} + (1.2)^3 \begin{bmatrix} 1 \\ -2 \\ 1 \end{bmatrix} = \begin{bmatrix} 18.5 \\ 23.3 \\ 18.5 \end{bmatrix} + \begin{bmatrix} 1.7 \\ -2.5 \\ 1.7 \end{bmatrix}$$

$\cdots$

6.6. References

[1] Kemeny, John G., and J. Laurie Snell, *Mathematical Models in the Social Sciences* (Boston: Ginn and Co., 1962), pp. 66–77.
[2] Rogers, Andrei, "A Markovian Policy Model of Interregional Migration," *Papers of the Regional Science Association*, XVII (1966), 205–224.

7 MIGRATION

7.1. Introduction

Over the past twenty years, quantitative models of internal migration have received considerable attention in the social sciences, particularly in the areas of sociology and demography. Much data have been collected, and numerous mathematical models have been proposed to account for apparent empirical regularities. These indicate that migration is a clearly patterned, nonrandom phenomenon which is subject to scientific explanation and, therefore, perhaps ultimately may be forecast with a reasonable degree of accuracy.

Internal migration may be approached from two different points of view: from the point of view of *migration streams* and from the point of view of *migration differentials*. These are not mutually exclusive conceptualizations, but each concentrates on a particular aspect of migration. Migration stream analyses focus on the volume and direction of place-to-place movements. Analyses of migration differentials select as their principal subject of inquiry the differences between migrant sub-groups. Whereas analyses of streams are concerned primarily with the effect that variations in environmental conditions at origins and destinations have on volumes of flow, studies of differentials are concerned with the traits of migrants in various age-sex-income-race classifications.

7.2. Analysis of Migration Streams

Economists repeatedly have asserted that the labor market allocates workers more or less where they belong in terms of their productive ability. Comparative economic opportunity, they argue, is the driving motivating force which is manifested in interregional migration patterns. According to this thesis, employment, occupation, and salary are the major considerations in any decision to move. In short, internal migration is held to be an important way by which people respond to changing economic opportunities and thereby redirect the spatial allocation of labor toward a more optimal pattern.

In the following paragraphs, we attempt to test this hypothesis by statistically measuring the degree of association between spatial variations in economic opportunities and variations in interregional migration flows in California. The migration data used for empirical testing are the U.S. Census reported 1955–1960 inter-SEA flows.[1]

Migration Streams and Economic Opportunity

Several models have been suggested for tests of the economic "push-pull" hypothesis. Of those currently available, the Lowry model appears to be conceptually most satisfactory.[2] This model is of the following form:

(7.1) $$M_{ij} = k \left[\frac{U_i}{U_j} \cdot \frac{W_j}{W_i} \cdot \frac{L_i L_j}{D_{ij}} \right] \xi_{ij},$$

or in its generalized log-transformed form:

(7.2) $$\ln M_{ij} = \beta_0 + \beta_1 \ln U_i + \beta_2 \ln U_j + \beta_3 \ln W_i + \beta_4 \ln W_j + \beta_5 \ln L_i + \beta_6 \ln L_j + \beta_7 \ln D_{ij} + \epsilon_{ij}$$

where M_{ij} = number of migrants from i to j;
L_i, L_j = number of persons in the nonagricultural labor force at i and j, respectively;
U_i, U_j = unemployment as a percentage of the civilian, nonagricultural labor force at i and j, respectively;
W_i, W_j = hourly manufacturing wage (in dollars and cents) at i and j, respectively;
D_{ij} = airline distance (in miles) separating i and j; and
ϵ_{ij} = error term.

---

[1] U.S. Bureau of the Census (PC(2)-2B), *U.S. Census of Population, 1960, Mobility for States and State Economic Areas*, U.S. Bureau of the Census, Department of Commerce, 1963.

[2] Ira S. Lowry, *Migration and Metropolitan Growth: Two Analytical Models* (San Francisco, Cal.: Chandler, 1966).

Migration

Thus, in matrix form, we have.

(7.3) $$\mathbf{y} = X\boldsymbol{\beta} + \boldsymbol{\epsilon}$$

where

$$\underset{m(m-1)\times 1}{\mathbf{y}} = \begin{bmatrix} \ln M_{12} \\ \ln M_{13} \\ \cdot \\ \cdot \\ \cdot \\ \ln M_{1m} \\ \hline \ln M_{21} \\ \cdot \\ \cdot \\ \cdot \\ \hline \cdot \\ \cdot \\ \cdot \\ \hline \ln M_{m1} \\ \cdot \\ \cdot \\ \ln M_{m,m-1} \end{bmatrix} \quad \underset{m(m-1)\times 1}{\boldsymbol{\epsilon}} = \begin{bmatrix} \epsilon_{12} \\ \epsilon_{13} \\ \cdot \\ \cdot \\ \cdot \\ \epsilon_{1m} \\ \hline \epsilon_{21} \\ \cdot \\ \cdot \\ \cdot \\ \hline \cdot \\ \cdot \\ \cdot \\ \hline \epsilon_{m1} \\ \cdot \\ \cdot \\ \epsilon_{m,m-1} \end{bmatrix} \quad \underset{8\times 1}{\boldsymbol{\beta}} = \begin{bmatrix} \beta_0 \\ \beta_1 \\ \beta_2 \\ \beta_3 \\ \beta_4 \\ \beta_5 \\ \beta_6 \\ \beta_7 \end{bmatrix}$$

and

$$\underset{m(m-1)\times 8}{X} = \begin{bmatrix} 1 & \ln U_1 & \ln U_2 & \ln W_1 & \ln W_2 & \ln L_1 & \ln L_2 & \ln D_{12} \\ 1 & \ln U_1 & \ln U_3 & \ln W_1 & \ln W_3 & \ln L_1 & \ln L_3 & \ln D_{13} \\ \cdot & \cdot & \cdot & \cdot & \cdot & \cdot & \cdot & \cdot \\ \cdot & \cdot & \cdot & \cdot & \cdot & \cdot & \cdot & \cdot \\ 1 & \ln U_1 & \ln U_m & \ln W_1 & \ln W_m & \ln L_1 & \ln L_m & \ln D_{lm} \\ \hline 1 & \ln U_2 & \ln U_1 & \ln W_2 & \ln W_1 & \ln L_2 & \ln L_1 & \ln D_{21} \\ \cdot & \cdot & \cdot & \cdot & \cdot & \cdot & \cdot & \cdot \\ \cdot & \cdot & \cdot & \cdot & \cdot & \cdot & \cdot & \cdot \\ \hline \cdot & \cdot & \cdot & \cdot & \cdot & \cdot & \cdot & \cdot \\ \cdot & \cdot & \cdot & \cdot & \cdot & \cdot & \cdot & \cdot \\ \hline 1 & \ln U_m & \ln U_1 & \ln W_m & \ln W_1 & \ln L_m & \ln L_1 & \ln D_{m1} \\ \cdot & \cdot & \cdot & \cdot & \cdot & \cdot & \cdot & \cdot \\ 1 & \ln U_m & \ln U_{m-1} & \ln W_m & \ln W_{m-1} & \ln L_m & \ln L_{m-1} & \ln D_{m,m-1} \end{bmatrix}$$

For testing the statistical fit of this model to inter-SMSA flows in California, a few modifications have been made in the operational definitions of the variables.[3] These reflect the significant role that agriculture holds in several of the regions analyzed. Thus in our version of Lowry's model:

L_i, L_j = number of persons in the civilian labor force at i and j, respectively; and

U_i, U_j = unemployment as a percentage of the civilian labor force at i and j, respectively.

Another modification is the redefinition of distance. Our D_{ij} is a measure of the shortest highway mileage separating the major county seats at i and j. In intrastate movements one would expect this to be a more accurate reflection of the "friction" of distance.

Recalling that the least squares estimator of β is

(7.4) $$\mathbf{b} = (X'X)^{-1}X'\mathbf{y},$$

we may proceed to derive the parameter estimates for the "modified" Lowry model defined in (7.3). Table 7.1A presents these estimates, indicates their significance, and lists the partial correlation coefficients and Coefficient of Determination. The fit of the model is impressive. Over 90 percent of the variation is accounted for by the seven variables, of which four are significantly different from zero at the 5 percent confidence level. Five of the seven variables have the signs which one would expect on *a priori* grounds. Migration from i to j is directly related to high wages at j and a large civilian labor force at either origin or destination. It is inversely related to high wages at i and increasing distance between i and j. The coefficients of unemployment rates at i and j should, on *a priori* grounds, be positive and negative, respectively. Their signs are reversed in Table 7.1. Neither is statistically significant, however.

The use of the Lowry model for forecasting purposes presents several problems. First, it requires as inputs average values over

---

[3] Data for Santa Barbara were incomplete and therefore flows from and to that SMSA were not included in the analysis. This reduced the number of observations from 90 to 72.

TABLE 7.1. REGRESSION STATISTICS FOR THE MODIFIED LOWRY MODEL

	A. Averages of 1955–1960 values for independent variables			B. 1955 values for independent variables		
Variable	Coefficient		Partial correlation coefficient	Variable	Coefficient	Partial correlation coefficient
Constant	−11.5133			Constant	−12.7369	
$\log L_i$	0.79578***		0.87806	$\log L_i$	0.79120***	0.87583
$\log L_j$	0.73608***		0.86157	$\log L_j$	0.76196***	0.86796
$\log D_{ij}$	−0.70688***		−0.78583	$\log D_{ij}$	−0.68717***	−0.77657
$\log W_j$	5.08408*		0.36842	$\log U_j$	1.43190***	0.47725
$\log U_j$	1.16108		0.22742	$\log W_j$	3.72478*	0.28981
$\log U_i$	−0.58726		−0.11730	$\log W_i$	1.07927	0.08740
$\log W_i$	−1.15274		−0.08949	$\log U_i$	−0.15494	−0.05866
R^2	0.90680			R^2	0.90547	

* Significantly different from zero at the 5% confidence level.
*** Significantly different from zero at the 0.1% confidence level.

the forecasting period for most of the independent variables. In a recursive model, operating with five-year increments, this presents a problem. For example, one would need to specify the average labor force over the next five-year period in order to generate the migrant flows during the same time interval. With a recursive structure it is much more convenient to be able to use the outputs of the current time period to generate the flows for the subsequent interval. Thus, in place of average values, we suggest the use of values for previous points in time. More specifically, we propose the use of 1955 status variables to forecast 1955–1960 flows instead of using averages over the five-year period. This modification of Lowry's model produces results that appear in Table 7.1B.

It is immediately apparent that the use of 1955 values for the independent variables in the Lowry model does not seriously affect the "goodness-of-fit" of the model. The R^2 remains virtually unchanged. Indeed an additional explanatory variable, the civilian unemployment rate at the destination, achieves significance. However, as before, its sign is the opposite of what one would expect from *a priori* reasoning.

Another problem which presents itself in any attempt to use the Lowry model as a forecasting tool is the need for forecasts of labor force totals. Within the framework of a cohort-survival projection model it is much more convenient to use the number of people in the 15–64 age group as a proxy. This segment of an area's population may be defined as "labor force eligibles." Moreover, to fit the Lowry model to inter-SEA flows in California one would require data on hourly manufacturing wage rates in nonmetropolitan subregions. This information is not currently available. As a proxy we suggest the use of per capita wages and salaries. These changes yield a model which we shall refer to as the Lowry-Rogers model:

$$(7.5) \qquad M_{ij} = k \left[\frac{U_i}{U_j} \cdot \frac{WS_j}{WS_i} \cdot \frac{LF_i \cdot LF_j}{D_{ij}} \right] \xi_{ij},$$

or in its generalized log-transformed form:

$$(7.6) \quad \ln M_{ij} = \beta_0 + \beta_1 \ln U_i + \beta_2 \ln U_j + \beta_3 \ln WS_i + \beta_4 \ln WS_j + \beta_5 \ln LF_i + \beta_6 \ln LF_j + \beta_7 \ln D_{ij} + \epsilon_{ij}$$

Migration

where M_{ij} = number of migrants from i to j;
U_i, U_j = civilian unemployment rate at i and j, respectively;
LF_i, LF_j = labor force eligibles at i and j, respectively;
WS_i, WS_j = per capita wages and salaries at i and j, respectively;
D_{ij} = shortest highway mileage between the major county seats at i and j, respectively; and
ϵ_{ij} = error term.

Fitting (7.6) to the same set of flows as were fitted by (7.2), we obtain the results shown in Table 7.2. It appears that a higher

TABLE 7.2. REGRESSION STATISTICS FOR THE LOWRY-ROGERS MODEL

Variable	Coefficient	Partial correlation coefficient
Constant	−10.8427	
log LF_i	0.88427***	0.84628
log LF_j	0.74402***	0.80071
log D_{ij}	−0.73903***	−0.82692
log U_j	1.15472***	0.46413
log WS_j	0.66320	0.20751
log WS_i	−0.56814	−0.17879
log U_i	−0.26044	−0.11737
R^2		0.92306

*** Significant at the 0.1% level.

explanatory power is achieved by the Lowry-Rogers model than by the "modified" Lowry model. Also it is interesting to note that the order in which the seven variables enter the stepwise regression program remains unchanged, and the same four variables are significant at the 0.1 percent level. Thus one may conclude that the Lowry-Rogers model, with its "proxy" variables, is a satisfactory alternative to the Lowry model.

In all of the three sets of regression statistics presented so far, the coefficients of the unemployment variables at i and j have the opposite sign than one would expect on *a priori* grounds. Since in two instances the unemployment rate at *j* is highly significant, this result is disturbing. More distressing, however, is the absence of a reasonable explanation for this finding. Because of the unexplainable behavior of the unemployment variable, we have removed it from the model, leaving us with what we shall refer to as the Rogers model:

$$(7.7) \qquad M_{ij} = k \left[\frac{WS_j}{WS_i} \cdot \frac{LF_i \cdot LF_j}{D_{ij}} \right] \xi_{ij},$$

or in its generalized log-transformed form:

$$(7.8) \qquad \ln M_{ij} = \beta_0 + \beta_1 \ln WS_i + \beta_2 \ln WS_j + \beta_3 \ln LF_i + \beta_4 \ln LF_j + \beta_5 \ln D_{ij} + \epsilon_{ij}$$

where M_{ij} = number of migrants from *i* to *j*;
LF_i, LF_j = labor force eligibles at *i* and *j*, respectively;
WS_i, WS_j = per capita wages and salaries at *i* and *j*, respectively;
D_{ij} = shortest highway mileage between the major county seats at *i* and *j*, respectively; and
ϵ_{ij} = error term.

In fitting the Rogers model to inter-SMSA flows (9 SMSA's, 72 observations) and then to the full matrix of inter-SEA flows (19 SEA's, 342 observations), we obtain the regression statistics presented in Table 7.3. These indicate a very slight decline in explanatory power with the R^2 dropping from the previous high of 0.92306 to 0.89930. The extension of the model to include non-SMSA flows results in a further decline of the R^2 to 0.80451. This, however, is a direct result of an increased number of observations and the mixing of metropolitan and nonmetropolitan flows. To see this more clearly let us now turn to an analysis of migration streams differentiated by class of subregion at origin and destination.

Migration Streams by Class of Subregion at Origin and Destination

Demographers have found considerable empirical support for the thesis that factors determining out-migration tend to vary

TABLE 7.3. REGRESSION STATISTICS FOR THE ROGERS MODEL

Variable	A. Fitted to 9×9 SMSA flow matrix		B. Fitted to 19×19 SEA flow matrix	
	Coefficient	Partial correlation coefficient	Coefficient	Partial correlation coefficient
Constant	−8.85352		−6.22950	
$\log LF_i$	0.90427***	0.83042	0.77237***	0.67441
$\log LF_j$	0.65533***	0.73382	0.68433***	0.62908
$\log D_{ij}$	−0.73790***	−0.78883	−0.80576***	−0.66157
$\log WS_i$	0.69195	0.18996	0.27159	0.06692
$\log WS_j$	−0.57479	−0.15869	−0.27132	−0.06686
R^2	0.89930		0.80451	

*** Significant at the 0.1% level.

with the type of destination as well as with the type of origin.[4] As a limited test of this hypothesis, we report, in Tables 7.4 and 7.5, the fit of the Rogers model to the 1955–1960 flow matrix, partitioned by metropolitan and nonmetropolitan origins and destinations.

Several interesting findings are indicated by the regression statistics. First, it is clear that the model provides a better accounting of flows originating from metropolitan subregions. This may be a reflection of the higher quality of information concerning economic opportunities that exists in metropolitan areas.[5] Second, per capita wages and salaries are significant only in flows to nonmetropolitan subregions. This suggests that people will not move to nonmetropolitan areas unless a definite improvement in per capita earnings is anticipated. Finally, it is encouraging to note that all five variables have signs which one would expect from *a priori* considerations. Migration from i to j is directly proportional to per capita wages at j and the product of the "masses" at i and j (as measured by labor force eligibles). It is inversely proportional to per capita wages and salaries at i and to the distance separating i and j.

7.3 Analysis of Migration Differentials

The definitive work on migration differentials continues to be that of Dorothy S. Thomas, whose exhaustive findings on this topic were published almost thirty years ago.[6] Since that time several significant analyses of migration differentials have appeared. Bogue and Hagood, by cross-classifying stream characteristics, simultaneously consider the joint effects of income, age, occupation, employment, marital status, and education on migration.[7] Beshers and Nishiura suggest a theory of internal

---

[4] See, for example, Donald J. Bogue, Henry S. Shryock, Jr., and Siegfried A. Hoermann, *Subregional Migration in the United States: 1935–40*, Vol. I (Oxford, Ohio: Scripps Foundation Studies in Population Distribution, Miami University, 1957).

[5] See: Phillip Nelson, "Migration, Real Income and Information," *Journal of Regional Science*, 1, No. 2 (Spring 1959), 43–62.

[6] Dorothy S. Thomas, *Research Memorandum on Migration Differentials* (New York: Social Science Research Council, 1938), Bulletin 43.

[7] Donald J. Bogue and Margaret Jarman Hagood, *Differential Migration in the Corn and Cotton Belts* (Oxford, Ohio: Scripps Foundation, 1953).

TABLE 7.4. REGRESSION STATISTICS FOR FLOWS FROM METROPOLITAN SUBREGIONS

	A. Flows from SMSA to SMSA subregions (10 × 10)		B. Flows from SMSA to non-SMSA subregions (10 × 9)	
Variable	Coefficient	Partial correlation coefficient	Coefficient	Partial correlation coefficient
Constant	−9.95275		−15.6364	
$\log LF_i$	0.92951***	0.76319	0.84771***	0.75224
$\log LF_j$	0.66109***	0.64320	−0.90221***	−0.78558
$\log D_{ij}$	−0.63601***	−0.64835	1.25055***	0.73883
$\log WS_j$	0.57868	0.12368	1.16687***	0.36380
$\log WS_i$	−0.44091	−0.09453	−0.81509	−0.18396
R^2	0.86651		0.85764	

*** Significant at the 0.1% level.

TABLE 7.5. Regression Statistics for Flows from Nonmetropolitan Subregions

	A. Flows from non-SMSA to non-SMSA subregions (9 × 9)			B. Flows from non-SMSA to SMSA subregions (9 × 10)	
Variable	Coefficient	Partial correlation coefficient	Variable	Coefficient	Partial correlation coefficient
Constant	−26.5621		Constant	−8.70549	
$\log D_{ij}$	−1.25719***	−0.62095	$\log LF_j$	0.56641***	0.56191
$\log LF_j$	1.29292***	0.62548	$\log D_{ij}$	−0.77613***	−0.69778
$\log LF_i$	0.85610***	0.46885	$\log LF_i$	0.77191***	0.51609
$\log WS_j$	1.25664**	0.32544	$\log WS_j$	0.49537	0.10077
$\log WS_i$	0.90810*	0.24136	$\log WS_i$	0.04996	0.01489
R^2	0.78592		R^2	0.76216	

* Significant at the 5% level.
** Significant at the 1% level.
*** Significant at the 0.1% level.

migration differentials.⁸ The principal hypotheses which consistently reappear in these and other studies are:

1. Young adults are the most mobile segment of the population.
2. Males tend to be more migratory than females.
3. Unemployed persons are more likely to move than employed persons.
4. Whites move more than nonwhites.
5. Professionals are among the most mobile elements of the population.

Paralleling the growing interest in quantitative analysis of migration phenomena has been the emergence of Markov chain theory as a methodological tool for analyzing social, industrial, and geographic mobility. Markov chains have been used to examine intergenerational mobility,⁹ to study the movement of workers between industries,¹⁰ and to project future population totals for Census Divisions in the United States.¹¹ By and large, however, the empirical results have been disappointing. What at first appeared to be a powerful new technique for temporal analysis has been found to be generally inapplicable in much of sociological and demographic research. Fundamentally, the discouraging results stem from the restrictive assumption of unchanging movement probabilities. Such an assumption, of course, is unrealistic in light of our knowledge concerning mobility in general and

---

⁸ James M. Beshers and Eleanor N. Nishuira, "A Theory of Internal Migration Differentials," *Social Forces*, 39 (1961), 214–218.

⁹ S. J. Prais, "Measuring Social Mobility," *Journal of the Royal Statistical Society*, Series A (1955), 56–66; John G. Kemeny and J. Laurie Snell, *Finite Markov Chains* (Princeton, N.J.: D. Van Nostrand Co., 1960), pp. 191–200.

¹⁰ Isadore Blumen, Marvin Kogan, and Philip J. McCarthy, *The Industrial Mobility of Labor as a Probability Process*, Vol. VI, Cornell Studies of Industrial and Labor Relations (Ithaca, New York: The New York State School of Industrial and Labor Relations, Cornell University, 1955).

¹¹ James D. Tarver and William R. Gurley, "A Stochastic Analysis of Geographic Mobility and Population Projections of the Census Divisions in the United States," *Demography*, II (1965), 134–139. See also: Robert McGinnis and John E. Pilger, "On a Model for Temporal Analysis," paper presented at the 58th Annual Meeting of the American Sociological Association, Los Angeles, August 29, 1963.

interregional migration in particular. Transition probabilities vary over time as well as over space. Moreover they are dependent on differential socioeconomic, demographic, and political situations at origins and destinations. Thus one may justifiably conclude that Markov chain models may be more useful in analyses of past migration flows and of very little practical use in efforts to forecast future place-to-place movements. However, though of limited utility in *temporal analysis*, it appears that Markovian concepts do provide useful indices for purposes of *differential analysis*. Thus despite its limited success in accounting for interregional migration streams, Markov chain theory does supply useful insights concerning the observed differential behavior of a population of migrant cohorts at a given point in time.

This section describes an investigation of migration differentials in California. The data are the U.S. Census reported flows for the 1955–1960 time period and supplementary estimates provided by a recent study completed for the California State Development Plan.[12] The method of analysis utilizes the Markovian concepts of transition matrices, mean first passage times, and equilibrium distributions.

Markovian Analysis of Migration Differentials

Consider an interregional system of m regions and a population composed of n cohorts. Define a cohort as a group of persons who behave independently but according to an identical migration structure. That is, assume that a member of cohort r behaves independently of all other members and according to an m by m transition matrix P_r. Then we may estimate each element of P_r by means of observed proportions taken over a cohort class, i.e.,

$$(7.9) \qquad {}_r p_{ij} = \frac{{}_r k_{ij}}{\sum_{j=1}^{m} {}_r k_{ij}}, \qquad \begin{array}{l}(r = 1, 2, \ldots, n) \\ (i, j = 1, 2, \ldots, m)\end{array}$$

where k_{ij} = the number of people, who during a specified time period, moved from region i to region j.

---

[12] Andrei Rogers, *An Analysis of Interregional Migration in California*, Center for Planning and Development Research, University of California, Berkeley, California, December 1965. See, for example, Figure 3.2.

Migration

With cohort-specific data on migration propensities, we may begin to study the changes of state that a single individual is likely to undergo in light of the transition structure of his cohort class. More specifically, for each cohort we may identify current movement characteristics and thereby establish a series of intra-cohort contrasts. Three properties of transition structures serve as particularly useful indices: the cohort's transition matrix, the associated mean first passage time matrix, and the equilibrium vector.

Transition Matrices.—Cohort-specific transition matrices provide a great deal of information about the mobility of migrant classes. In particular, their diagonal elements provide an immediate dimension along which we may contrast the degree of overall mobility of different migrant groups. For example, consider a hypothetical system of only two regions, A and B, and a population divided into two broad cohort classes, white and nonwhite. Let us suppose that if an individual, in the white cohort class, is in region A, there is a 50 percent chance that he will move to region B during the unit time interval. If the person is currently in region B, however, with probability $\frac{1}{4}$ he will move to A during the same time period. Assume, further, that for the nonwhite cohort class the corresponding probabilities are $\frac{1}{4}$ and $\frac{1}{5}$. In matrix form, we have then:

$$P_W = \begin{matrix} & \begin{matrix} A & B \end{matrix} \\ \begin{matrix} A \\ B \end{matrix} & \begin{bmatrix} \frac{1}{2} & \frac{1}{2} \\ \frac{1}{4} & \frac{3}{4} \end{bmatrix} \end{matrix} \qquad P_{NW} = \begin{matrix} & \begin{matrix} A & B \end{matrix} \\ \begin{matrix} A \\ B \end{matrix} & \begin{bmatrix} \frac{3}{4} & \frac{1}{4} \\ \frac{1}{5} & \frac{4}{5} \end{bmatrix} \end{matrix}.$$

Immediately we observe that the diagonal elements of P_{NW} are greater than the corresponding entries in P_W. From this we may infer that nonwhites are *less* mobile than whites. If our interregional system contained more than two regions, we would, in addition, be in a position to compare the relative "attraction" of alternative destinations for different migrant cohorts.

Mean First Passage Times.—Frequently it is desirable to study the length of time it takes an average individual to move from state i to state j for the first time. The distribution describing this random variable is called the first passage time distribution. Its mean is commonly referred to as the mean first passage time.

Turning to our two-region example, consider the probability

that an individual currently in region A will move to region B, *for the first time*, in n time periods. Denote this probability by $g_{AB}^{(n)}$ and begin with n equal to 1. Then,

$$g_A{}^{(1)}{}_B = p_{AB}$$
$$g_{AB}^{(2)} = p_{AA} \cdot p_{AB}$$

and, by substitution,

$$g_{AB}^{(2)} = p_{AA} g_{AB}^{(1)}.$$

The above equations merely state that an individual's probability of going from A to B, *for the first time*, in one time period is p_{AB} (by definition), and the probability of doing this in two steps is the product of the probability of remaining in A during the first time period and the probability of moving to B during the second.

Extending the argument to the general case, for this two-region example, we have:

(7.10)
$$\begin{aligned} g_{AB}^{(n)} &= p_{AA} \cdot g_{AB}^{(n-1)} \\ &= p_{AA} \cdot p_{AA} \cdot g_{AB}^{(n-2)} \\ &= \ldots \\ &= (p_{AA})^{n-1} \cdot p_{AB}. \end{aligned}$$

This function is called the first passage time distribution. Since $p_{AA} = 1 - p_{AB}$, we have

(7.11) $$g_{AB}^{(n)} = p_{AB}(1 - p_{AB})^{n-1}$$

which is the geometric distribution of elementary probability theory with a mean

(7.12) $$m_{AB} = \frac{1}{p_{AB}}.$$

This statistic is defined as the mean first passage time and represents the average number of time periods required for a person in region A to visit region B for the first time. The matrix M, consisting of entries m_{ij}, is defined as the mean first passage time matrix.

Returning to our numerical example, we find for the white cohort:

$$g_{AB}^{(n)} = (\tfrac{1}{2})(\tfrac{1}{2})^{n-1}$$

and

$$m_{AB} = \frac{1}{\tfrac{1}{2}} = 2.$$

In general, the mean first passage times of a Markov chain may be found by recursively applying the following equation:

(7.13) $$m_{ij} = p_{ij} + \sum_{k \neq 1} p_{ik}m_{ki}.$$ [13]

Kemeny and Snell, however, offer a more convenient matrix formulation:

(7.14) $$M = (I - Z + EZ_{dg})D,$$

where D = a diagonal matrix with elements $d_{ii} = 1/a_i$;
 E = a matrix with all elements equal to 1;
 I = the identity matrix;
 Z = the fundamental matrix;
 Z_{dg} = the Z matrix with all off-diagonal entries set equal to 0.

The fundamental matrix, Z, is defined by the following equation:

(7.15) $$Z = [I - (P - A)]^{-1},$$

where P = the matrix of transition probabilities;
 A = a matrix with each row identically equal to the equilibrium vector **a**.

The computation of the matrix of mean first passage times may be illustrated by returning to our example:

$$Z_W = \left\{ \begin{bmatrix} 1 & 0 \\ 0 & 1 \end{bmatrix} - \left(\begin{bmatrix} \frac{1}{2} & \frac{1}{2} \\ \frac{1}{4} & \frac{3}{4} \end{bmatrix} - \begin{bmatrix} \frac{1}{3} & \frac{2}{3} \\ \frac{1}{3} & \frac{2}{3} \end{bmatrix} \right) \right\}^{-1}$$

$$= \begin{bmatrix} \frac{5}{6} & \frac{1}{6} \\ \frac{1}{12} & \frac{11}{12} \end{bmatrix}^{-1}$$

$$= \begin{bmatrix} \frac{11}{9} & -\frac{2}{9} \\ -\frac{1}{9} & \frac{10}{9} \end{bmatrix},$$

and

$$M_W = \left(\begin{bmatrix} 1 & 0 \\ 0 & 1 \end{bmatrix} - \begin{bmatrix} \frac{11}{9} & -\frac{2}{9} \\ -\frac{1}{9} & \frac{10}{9} \end{bmatrix} + \begin{bmatrix} 1 & 1 \\ 1 & 1 \end{bmatrix} \begin{bmatrix} \frac{11}{9} & 0 \\ 0 & \frac{10}{9} \end{bmatrix} \right) \begin{bmatrix} 3 & 0 \\ 0 & 1\frac{1}{2} \end{bmatrix}$$

$$= \begin{bmatrix} 3 & 2 \\ 4 & 1\frac{1}{2} \end{bmatrix}.$$

[13] For a derivation of this equation, see: John G. Kemeny and J. Laurie Snell, *op. cit.*, pp. 78–80. Their notation has been retained in order to avoid confusion.

As a check, notice that m_{12} is again equal to 2.

Repeating the above computation for the nonwhite cohort, we have:

$$M_{NW} = \begin{bmatrix} 2\frac{1}{4} & 4 \\ 5 & 1\frac{4}{9} \end{bmatrix}.$$

Mean first passage times provide a measure of a particular kind of contiguity—one based on interchange probabilities rather than distance. Thus they may be viewed as indices of aspatial interregional distance. Let us define this aspatial measure of proximity as "migrant distance."

With reference to our two-region, two-cohort example we may make both an intra-cohort observation and an inter-cohort contrast:

(1) "Migrant distance" from region A to region B, for both cohorts, is "shorter" than the distance from B to A. This asymmetry suggests that, on the basis of actual migrant exchange, B is "closer" to the population at A than A is to the population at B.

(2) White "migrant distance" from region A to region B is "shorter" than nonwhite "migrant distance" between the same two regions.

Equilibrium Distributions.—The transition matrix P provides a great deal of information about the Markovian migration process described above. For example, it allows us to derive the probability that an individual currently residing in region A will be in region B after 2 years. This "event" can occur only by one of two mutually exclusive and collectively exhaustive ways:

(1) the individual remains in A during the first year and migrates to B during the second year;

(2) the individual migrates to B during the first year and remains in B during the second year.

Therefore, for the white cohort,

$$\begin{aligned} p_{AB}{}^{(2)} &= p_{AA}p_{AB} + p_{AB}p_{BB} \\ &= (\tfrac{1}{2})(\tfrac{1}{2}) + (\tfrac{1}{2})(\tfrac{3}{4}) \\ &= \tfrac{5}{8}. \end{aligned}$$

With analogous arguments we find:

$$p_{AA}{}^{(2)} = (\tfrac{1}{2})(\tfrac{1}{2}) + (\tfrac{1}{2})(\tfrac{1}{4}) = \tfrac{3}{8},$$

Migration

$$p_{BA}{}^{(2)} = (\tfrac{1}{4})(\tfrac{1}{2}) + (\tfrac{3}{4})(\tfrac{1}{4}) = \tfrac{5}{16},$$
$$p_{BB}{}^{(2)} = (\tfrac{1}{4})(\tfrac{1}{2}) + (\tfrac{3}{4})(\tfrac{3}{4}) = \tfrac{11}{16}.$$

These numbers can be presented in a matrix:

$$P_W{}^{(2)} = \begin{array}{c} \\ A \\ B \end{array} \begin{array}{cc} A & B \\ \begin{bmatrix} \tfrac{3}{8} & \tfrac{5}{8} \\ \tfrac{5}{16} & \tfrac{11}{16} \end{bmatrix} \end{array}.$$

The matrix $P^{(2)}$ describes movement between two periods of time. Similarly $P^{(n)}$ describes movement during n time periods. It should now become apparent that the transition matrix P, in a Markov chain model, completely determines the character of the migration process. Therefore, it is possible to use these short-term data to compare the movement patterns of different classes of individuals, to project these into the future, and to assess what are the intrinsic distributional consequences of a particular movement structure.

The essential feature of representing Markov processes by transition matrices stems from the ease with which nth order transition probabilities may be derived by matrix multiplication. In particular, the multiplication of the transition probability matrix P by itself, n number of times, yields the nth-order transition probabilities. For example, it can be shown that:

$$P^{(2)} = P \cdot P = P^2,$$

and, in general,

(7.16) $$P^{(n)} = P^n.$$

This can be demonstrated by our example:

$$P_W = \begin{bmatrix} \tfrac{1}{2} & \tfrac{1}{2} \\ \tfrac{1}{4} & \tfrac{3}{4} \end{bmatrix} = \begin{bmatrix} .50 & .50 \\ .25 & .75 \end{bmatrix}$$

$$P_W{}^2 = \begin{bmatrix} .38 & .62 \\ .31 & .69 \end{bmatrix}$$

$$P_W{}^3 = \begin{bmatrix} .34 & .66 \\ .33 & .67 \end{bmatrix}$$

$$P_W{}^5 = \begin{bmatrix} .33 & .67 \\ .33 & .67 \end{bmatrix} = \begin{bmatrix} \tfrac{1}{3} & \tfrac{2}{3} \\ \tfrac{1}{3} & \tfrac{2}{3} \end{bmatrix}.$$

Similarly, for the nonwhite cohort:

$$P_{NW}{}^8 = \begin{bmatrix} \tfrac{4}{9} & \tfrac{5}{9} \\ \tfrac{4}{9} & \tfrac{5}{9} \end{bmatrix}.$$

An interesting and very important feature of a class of Markov processes, defined as "ergodic" chains, is illustrated by the above matrices. It will be noted that initially the transition probabilities are different for each of the two states. That is, a migrant's destination is heavily influenced by his place of origin. However, after n powers of the transition matrix are calculated it becomes apparent that the effect of the starting state disappears. For example, for the white cohort this occurs when n is equal to 5. For this and larger values of n, the rows of the transition matrix are identical. This means that as n increases, $p_{ij}^{(n)}$, the probability of migrating from i to j in n years, approaches a limit p_j which is independent of i. At this point the system is said to be in "equilibrium" or to have reached a "steady state."[14]

Comparing the equilibrium vectors of the white and nonwhite cohorts in our example suggests something of the long-term implications of current behavior. It is an abstract index, to be sure, since "death" is not included as a possible end-state. Nevertheless, the steady state vector may be viewed as a kind of "speedometer" which describes the ultimate consequences of the current movement pattern if it remains unchanged. Instead of assuming that the driver doesn't die and that his car continues at exactly the same speed for an hour, we assume that the migrant doesn't die and that the transition probabilities remain constant.

In our example, we note that on the basis of current trends it appears that the white cohort is favoring region B as a destination. A similar observation may be made with respect to the nonwhite cohort.

Migration Differentials in California: Some Empirical Results

According to the Census of 1960, more than 2.1 million persons migrated to California between 1955 and 1960 while slightly less than a million departed, thus producing a net increase of some 1.2 million people over the five-year period.[15] Origins and destinations for these migrants, by 19 State Economic Areas, have

---

[14] This result follows from our discussion of the stability properties of nonnegative matrices in Chapter 5.

[15] Financial and Population Research Section, *California Migration: 1955–1960*, California Department of Finance, Sacramento, 1964, p. 1.

been published[16] and total age- and color-specific intrastate flows and transition matrices have been estimated.[17] For ease of exposition, however, we shall structure the discussion around selected matrices of a smaller order. In particular, we shall focus on the reduced versions which are exhibited in Tables 7.6 through 7.11.[18]

Transition Matrices.—Several interesting findings are suggested by the transition matrices. These are by no means surprising and, indeed, merely support relatively well-established demographic hypotheses.

First, it is clear that the transition probabilities have not remained constant over time. The population has become much more mobile both at the interstate and the intrastate levels. This is immediately apparent from even the most cursory examination of Table 7.6. In every instance the diagonal element of the 1935–1940 matrix is larger than the corresponding diagonal element of the 1955–1960 matrix. This points to the greater mobility of today's population. For example, for the 1935–1940 cohort, the probability that a member of the San Francisco–Oakland population moves out of that SMSA is less than 0.09. The corresponding figure for the 1955–1960 time interval is almost 0.15. The change for other SEA's is less striking, but is significant nevertheless.

Second, there are significant differences between the characteristics of white and nonwhite flow patterns. Nonwhite probabilities are considerably higher than white probabilities in urban to urban transfers and much lower in urban to suburban-rural movements. Every diagonal element of the nonwhite matrix in Table 7.7 is larger than the corresponding element of the white

---

[16] U.S. Bureau of the Census (PC(2)-2B), *U.S. Census of Population, 1960, Mobility for States and State Economic Areas*, U.S. Bureau of the Census, Department of Commerce, 1963.

[17] These were developed in the study: Andrei Rogers, *Projected Population Growth in California Regions: 1960–1980*, Center for Planning and Development Research, University of California, December 1965. For estimating procedures see pp. 15–17 of that study.

[18] Transition matrices for the 1935–1940 time period were derived from interregional flow data reported in: Donald J. Bogue, Henry S. Shryock, Jr., and Siegfried A. Hoermann, *Subregional Migration in the United States, 1935–40, Volume I: Streams of Migration* (Oxford, Ohio: Scripps Foundation, Miami University, 1957).

TABLE 7.6. Transition Matrices and Equilibrium Distributions for California: by Time Period*

A. 1935–1940 Total Flows

	A	B	C	F	G	CAL.	U.S.
A	.9139	.0067	.0049	.0615	.0022	.0293	.0265
B	.0575	.8529	.0056	.0121	.0034	.0459	.0226
C	.0379	.0030	.8434	.0125	.0019	.0741	.0272
F	.0096	.0012	.0013	.9215	.0058	.0242	.0364
G	.0147	.0014	.0043	.0498	.8371	.0208	.0719
CAL.	.0280	.0059	.0086	.0031	.0044	.8912	.0288
U.S.	.0009	.0001	.0001	.0033	.0004	.0020	.9932

Equilibrium Vector:

	A	B	C	F	G	CAL.	U.S.
a =	[.0387	.0050	.0053	.0688	.0065	.0479	.8279]

B. 1955–1960 Total Flows

	A	B	C	F	G	CAL.	U.S.
A	.8543	.0203	.0070	.0172	.0053	.0363	.0596
B	.0460	.8271	.0053	.0155	.0043	.0465	.0553
C	.0247	.0061	.8165	.0142	.0034	.0667	.0684
F	.0076	.0043	.0030	.8907	.0078	.0324	.0542
G	.0120	.0046	.0019	.0371	.7923	.0255	.1266
CAL.	.0209	.0099	.0109	.0327	.0078	.8538	.0640
U.S.	.0017	.0006	.0004	.0056	.0016	.0028	.9873

Equilibrium Vector:

	A	B	C	F	G	CAL.	U.S.
a =	[.0253	.0107	.0070	.0667	.0116	.0456	.8331]

*A = S.F.–Oakland; B = San Jose; C = Sacramento; F = Los Angeles; G = San Diego; CAL. = Rest of California; U.S. = Rest of the U.S.

matrix. For example, the probability that an individual of the nonwhite cohort in the Los Angeles-Long Beach SMSA moves out of that subregion during the 1955–1960 period is less than 0.06. The corresponding figure for whites is approximately twice that number. Nonwhite movements also are primarily urban to urban migrations. In Table 7.11 we note that nonwhite probabilities are relatively higher than probabilities in SMSA to

Migration

TABLE 7.7. Transition Matrices and Equilibrium Distributions for California: by Color

A. 1955–1960 White Flows

	A	B	C	F	G	CAL.	U.S.
A	.8465	.0221	.0073	.0172	.0056	.0388	.0625
B	.0453	.8269	.0053	.0154	.0044	.0465	.0562
C	.0247	.0063	.8118	.0141	.0035	.0689	.0707
F	.0077	.0046	.0032	.8863	.0082	.0339	.0561
G	.0117	.0048	.0019	.0367	.7897	.0260	.1292
CAL.	.0208	.0102	.0110	.0326	.0080	.8526	.0648
U.S.	.0018	.0006	.0004	.0058	.0017	.0030	.9867

Equilibrium Vector:

	A	B	C	F	G	CAL.	U.S.
a =	[.0249	.0112	.0071	.0661	.0121	.0477	.8309]

B. 1955–1960 Nonwhite Flows

	A	B	C	F	G	CAL.	U.S.
A	.9174	.0059	.0044	.0171	.0026	.0162	.0364
B	.0660	.8341	.0052	.0190	.0027	.0439	.0291
C	.0245	.0031	.8792	.0156	.0016	.0376	.0384
F	.0062	.0009	.0011	.9437	.0030	.0143	.0308
G	.0166	.0011	.0012	.0444	.8425	.0182	.0760
CAL.	.0234	.0048	.0095	.0356	.0058	.8728	.0481
U.S.	.0016	.0001	.0002	.0045	.0007	.0011	.9918

Equilibrium Vector:

	A	B	C	F	G	CAL.	U.S.
a =	[.0371	.0033	.0060	.1023	.0073	.0273	.8167]

SMSA movements, but are much lower in SMSA to non-SMSA transfers.

Finally, considerable differences appear to exist between the migration structures of various age groups. Tables 7.8, 7.9, and 7.10 highlight the age-specific mobility pattern which emerges out of an analysis of the transition matrices of the 17 age cohorts in California. Although considerable differences exist between individual SEA's, the overall distribution is unmistakable. The probability of leaving an SEA is highest for the 15- to 19- and 20- to 24-year age groups and lowest for the post-65-year age

TABLE 7.8. Transition Matrices and Equilibrium
Distributions for California:
by Age Group

A. 1955–1960 Flows for Age Group #2: 5 to 9 years

	A	B	C	F	G	CAL.	U.S.
A	.8458	.0215	.0074	.0182	.0056	.0384	.0631
B	.0469	.8238	.0054	.0158	.0044	.0473	.0564
C	.0256	.0063	.8101	.0147	.0035	.0690	.0708
F	.0081	.0046	.0032	.8834	.0083	.0346	.0578
G	.0116	.0045	.0018	.0358	.7997	.0245	.1221
CAL.	.0215	.0101	.0113	.0338	.0081	.8497	.0655
U.S.	.0016	.0005	.0004	.0050	.0014	.0025	.9886

Equilibrium Vector:

	A	B	C	F	G	CAL.	U.S.
a =	[.0223	.0095	.0064	.0573	.0109	.0408	.8527]

B. 1955–1960 Flows for Age Group #4: 15 to 19 years

	A	B	C	F	G	CAL.	U.S.
A	.6952	.0424	.0146	.0359	.0111	.0761	.1247
B	.0740	.7221	.0086	.0250	.0069	.0745	.0889
C	.0433	.0107	.6782	.0249	.0059	.1170	.1200
F	.0142	.0081	.0057	.7952	.0146	.0607	.1015
G	.0223	.0086	.0035	.0690	.6136	.0475	.2355
CAL.	.0334	.0167	.0168	.0518	.0123	.7668	.1022
U.S.	.0033	.0011	.0008	.0106	.0030	.0052	.9760

Equilibrium Vector:

	A	B	C	F	G	CAL.	U.S.
a =	[.0228	.0125	.0075	.0666	.0116	.0533	.8255]

groups. The distribution is unimodal and resembles the Gamma distribution. The high values are distributed around 0.40 with the low values approaching zero. The maximum is attained by the South Central Coast SEA. Here the probability that an individual in the 15- to 19-year age group moves out of this SEA is almost 0.44.

Mean First Passage Times.—Tables 7.12, 7.13, and 7.14 present mean first passage time matrices for six of the eight transition matrices appearing in Tables 7.6, 7.7, 7.9, and 7.10. The actual values of these "migrant distances" are quite meaningless, however, when considered in relative terms, they suggest several

Migration

TABLE 7.9. Transition Matrices and Equilibrium Distributions for California: by Age Group

A. *1955–1960 Flows for Age Group #5: 20 to 24 years*

	A	B	C	F	G	CAL.	U.S.
A	.7288	.0377	.0130	.0320	.0099	.0676	.1110
B	.0710	.7332	.0082	.0240	.0067	.0715	.0854
C	.0445	.0110	.6693	.0256	.0061	.1202	.1233
F	.0138	.0079	.0056	.8006	.0142	.0590	.0989
G	.0204	.0079	.0032	.0630	.6468	.0435	.2152
CAL.	.0324	.0161	.0164	.0531	.0127	.7668	.1025
U.S.	.0036	.0012	.0009	.0116	.0033	.0057	.9737

Equilibrium Vector:

	A	B	C	F	G	CAL.	U.S.
a =	[.0272	.0138	.0078	.0735	.0137	.0570	.8070]

B. *1955–1960 Flows for Age Group #8: 35 to 39 years*

	A	B	C	F	G	CAL.	U.S.
A	.8825	.0163	.0056	.0138	.0043	.0294	.0481
B	.0391	.8531	.0045	.0132	.0037	.0394	.0470
C	.0215	.0053	.8403	.0124	.0029	.0581	.0595
F	.0063	.0036	.0025	.9097	.0064	.0267	.0448
G	.0087	.0033	.0013	.0268	.8497	.0186	.0916
CAL.	.0186	.0086	.0099	.0291	.0069	.8701	.0568
U.S.	.0016	.0005	.0004	.0050	.0014	.0025	.9886

Equilibrium Vector:

	A	B	C	F	G	CAL.	U.S.
a =	[.0283	.0109	.0074	.0713	.0140	.0455	.8226]

interesting findings concerning spatial and aspatial contiguities among California's major SMSA's.

A quick glance at the 1935–1940 and 1955–1960 mean first passage time matrices reveals changes both in intra- and intermatrix levels. In general, it is clear that migrant distances declined over the twenty-year period—a reflection of increased geographical mobility. Other changes, however, are equally noteworthy. Perhaps the most noticeable is the shortening of migrant distances in relation to the distance between the Los Angeles–Long Beach and the San Francisco–Oakland SMSA's. For example, whereas during the 1935–1940 period the migrant distance

TABLE 7.10. Transition Matrices and Equilibrium Distributions for California: by Age Group

A. *1955–1960 Flows for Age Group #11: 50 to 54 years*

	A	B	C	F	G	CAL.	U.S.
A	.9293	.0098	.0034	.0083	.0026	.0177	.0289
B	.0256	.9038	.0030	.0086	.0024	.0258	.0308
C	.0130	.0032	.9034	.0075	.0018	.0351	.0360
F	.0043	.0025	.0017	.9378	.0044	.0185	.0308
G	.0053	.0020	.0008	.0163	.9090	.0111	.0555
CAL.	.0137	.0062	.0074	.0205	.0050	.9062	.0410
U.S.	.0008	.0003	.0002	.0026	.0007	.0013	.9941

Equilibrium Vector:

	A	B	C	F	G	CAL.	U.S.
a =	[.0252	.0094	.0067	.0557	.0123	.0341	.8566]

B. *1955–1960 Flows for Age Group #14: 65 to 69 years*

	A	B	C	F	G	CAL.	U.S.
A	.9383	.0086	.0030	.0073	.0023	.0152	.0253
B	.0228	.9145	.0027	.0077	.0021	.0228	.0274
C	.0108	.0026	.9195	.0063	.0015	.0292	.0301
F	.0038	.0022	.0015	.9456	.0039	.0160	.0270
G	.0046	.0018	.0007	.0142	.9206	.0097	.0484
CAL.	.0116	.0052	.0060	.0175	.0042	.9206	.0349
U.S.	.0007	.0002	.0002	.0021	.0006	.0011	.9951

Equilibrium Vector:

	A	B	C	F	G	CAL.	U.S.
a =	[.0245	.0083	.0069	.0525	.0119	.0336	.8622]

from Los Angeles to San Jose was over four times that of the migrant distance between Los Angeles and San Francisco, by 1955–1960 this ratio had declined to two to one.

Differences both within and between the white and nonwhite mean first passage time matrices are quite apparent in Table 7.13. Particularly striking are the nonwhite migrant distances to the San Jose SMSA. The nonwhite migrant distance between the San Francisco–Oakland and the San Jose SMSA's, for example, is nine times the reverse distance and thirteen times the distance between the San Francisco and the Los Angeles SMSA's.

TABLE 7.11. TRANSITION MATRICES AND EQUILIBRIUM DISTRIBUTIONS FOR CALIFORNIA: BY SMSA AND NON-SMSA FLOWS

A. Total Flows 1955–1960

	S.	N.S.	U.S.
SMSA	.9167	.0211	.0622
Non-SMSA	.1120	.8218	.0662
U.S.	.0114	.0013	.9873

Equilibrium Vector:

$a = [.1451 \quad .0232 \quad .8317]$

B. White Flows 1955–1960

	S.	N.S.	U.S.
SMSA	.9135	.0221	.0644
Non-SMSA	.1121	.8214	.0665
U.S.	.0119	.0014	.9867

$a = [.1459 \quad .0246 \quad .8295]$

C. Nonwhite Flows 1955–1960

	S.	N.S.	U.S.
SMSA	.9556	.0085	.0359
Non-SMSA	.1101	.8326	.0573
U.S.	.0077	.0005	.9918

$a = [.1695 \quad .0111 \quad .8194]$

D. Flows for 15–19 Age Group 1955–1960

	S.	N.S.	U.S.
SMSA	.8422	.0391	.1187
Non-SMSA	.1788	.7150	.1062
U.S.	.0215	.0025	.9760

Equilibrium Vector:

$a = [.1436 \quad .0270 \quad .8294]$

E. Flows for 35–39 Age Group 1955–1960

	S.	N.S.	U.S.
SMSA	.9319	.0175	.0506
Non-SMSA	.0995	.8416	.0589
U.S.	.0102	.0012	.9886

$a = [.1571 \quad .0236 \quad .8193]$

F. Flows for 50–54 Age Group 1955–1960

	S.	N.S.	U.S.
SMSA	.9554	.0114	.0332
Non-SMSA	.0708	.8873	.0419
U.S.	.0053	.0006	.9941

$a = [.1293 \quad .0176 \quad .8530]$

TABLE 7.12. Mean First Passage Times: by Time Period

A. *1935–1940 Total Flows*

	A	B	C	F	G	CAL.	U.S.
A	25.8	1304.2	1174.6	145.0	915.1	146.5	33.3
B	179.0	200.0	1161.7	145.5	915.0	127.2	34.1
C	215.8	1339.2	188.7	144.4	913.5	106.1	33.0
F	291.9	1400.9	1239.8	14.5	889.8	171.0	29.5
G	301.7	1416.0	1237.1	136.2	153.8	192.1	23.4
CAL.	238.1	1329.2	1154.7	128.6	898.8	20.9	32.2
U.S.	382.1	1492.7	1333.5	216.4	990.3	264.1	1.2

B. *1955–1960 Total Flows*

	A	B	C	F	G	CAL.	U.S.
A	39.5	485.2	749.8	119.3	398.0	118.1	16.3
B	204.9	93.5	753.8	119.4	399.3	110.6	16.6
C	238.0	530.2	142.9	120.8	402.2	102.1	15.4
F	264.1	541.2	771.3	15.0	389.0	121.3	16.8
G	271.5	554.3	791.3	116.1	86.2	143.1	11.2
CAL.	243.4	521.9	737.6	109.8	392.4	21.9	15.8
U.S.	300.1	583.8	817.2	143.0	421.7	174.5	1.2

TABLE 7.13. Mean First Passage Times: by Color

A. *1955–1960 White Flows*

	A	B	C	F	G	CAL.	U.S.
A	40.2	460.5	720.6	116.4	376.6	111.2	15.7
B	199.4	89.3	725.0	116.4	378.0	105.1	16.2
C	230.8	505.9	140.8	117.8	380.8	96.6	15.0
F	255.2	515.8	740.7	15.1	367.9	114.5	16.3
G	262.7	529.1	760.8	113.2	82.6	135.6	10.9
CAL.	235.6	497.5	709.0	107.0	371.3	21.0	15.4
U.S.	289.1	557.6	785.4	138.4	399.0	165.1	1.2

B. *1955–1960 Nonwhite Flows*

	A	B	C	F	G	CAL.	U.S.
A	27.0	1762.5	1335.1	135.9	846.2	248.0	27.1
B	190.1	303.0	1319.7	130.2	841.2	204.0	27.9
C	257.2	1810.4	166.7	136.0	851.3	207.8	26.3
F	309.6	1866.5	1388.2	9.8	838.8	252.4	29.1
G	303.5	1876.0	1400.6	123.7	137.0	270.4	20.7
CAL.	272.0	1808.0	1305.8	121.8	830.2	36.6	25.0
U.S.	363.0	1937.6	1455.0	180.3	890.0	339.3	1.2

Migration

TABLE 7.14. Mean First Passage Times: by Age Group

A. *1955–1960 Flows for Age Group #5: 20 to 24 years*

	A	B	C	F	G	CAL.	U.S.
A	36.8	243.3	373.2	59.3	198.3	58.7	9.2
B	103.1	72.5	375.9	59.9	199.5	55.6	10.0
C	119.1	265.8	128.2	60.1	200.5	50.8	8.9
F	132.0	271.3	383.7	13.6	193.9	60.4	9.6
G	135.3	277.7	393.3	57.6	73.0	71.0	6.5
CAL.	122.5	261.9	368.8	54.8	195.8	17.5	9.4
U.S.	148.5	291.7	404.8	70.0	209.1	85.9	1.2

B. *1955–1960 Flows for Age Group #14: 65 to 69 years*

	A	B	C	F	G	CAL.	U.S.
A	40.8	1267.0	1733.8	307.3	1011.1	298.7	35.3
B	497.2	120.5	1740.3	305.3	1013.4	277.8	34.2
C	580.2	1385.6	145.0	310.5	1022.2	257.7	32.8
F	641.0	1408.7	1781.9	19.0	986.1	303.6	34.2
G	664.6	1448.9	1833.5	301.8	84.0	363.0	25.7
CAL.	589.2	1361.9	1702.0	280.9	995.2	29.8	31.4
U.S.	736.6	1529.5	1893.7	373.0	1078.2	443.2	1.2

This may be a reflection of the racial discrimination in San Jose's housing market.

The mean first passage time matrices for the 20- to 24- and 65- to 69-year age groups differ considerably in absolute values but are very similar in relative terms. This is an indication that, although the former age group is much more mobile than the latter age group, their movement patterns are quite similar. For example, in both matrices the distance from San Jose to Sacramento is three times that of the reverse distance.

Finally, it is interesting to note the total absence of any significant correlation between interregional highway-mileage distances (Table 7.15) and interregional migrant distances as measured by mean first passage times. Table 7.16 presents the correlations between each of the mean first passage time matrices in Tables 7.12, 7.13, and 7.14 and the interregional distances shown in Table 7.15. Clearly the spatial and aspatial measures of interregional distances are totally unrelated.

Equilibrium Distributions.—The migration differentials revealed by the transition matrices in Tables 7.6, 7.7, 7.8, 7.9, 7.10, and

TABLE 7.15. INTERREGIONAL DISTANCES*

	A	B	C	F	G	CAL.	U.S.
A	—	48	89	403	522	—	—
B	48	—	125	366	485	—	—
C	89	125	—	383	502	—	—
F	403	366	383	—	120	—	—
G	522	485	502	120	—	—	—
CAL.	—	—	—	—	—	—	—
U.S.	—	—	—	—	—	—	—

* County seat to county seat highway mileages.

TABLE 7.16. CORRELATIONS BETWEEN INTERREGIONAL MEAN FIRST PASSAGE TIMES AND INTERREGIONAL DISTANCES*

	R
Temporal:	
1935–1940 matrix	.024
1955–1960 matrix	−.012
Color:	
White	−.015
Nonwhite	−.047
Age:	
20- to 24-year age group	−.014
65- to 69-year age group	−.005

* Computed on the basis of twenty observations.

7.11 are readily recognizable. Differences in the propensity to move are immediately apparent. Not so obvious, perhaps, are the implied distributional consequences of the various transition structures. For example, a comparison of the equilibrium vectors of the 1935–1940 and the 1955–1960 transition matrices suggests that California's attraction as a destination has declined slightly over the 20-year period. This is not immediately apparent from a consideration of the transition matrices alone.

At more disaggregated levels, the equilibrium solutions present a detailed, quantitative picture of the spatial implications of current mobility trends. Moreover, they provide indications of temporal changes and of differentials between migrant subclasses.

The temporal changes in the values of the equilibrium vectors

Migration

for California's population have little meaning other than as an index of the direction of changes in regional preferences over time. Perhaps the most significant finding in Table 7.6 is the decline in the equilibrium probabilities for the San Francisco–Oakland and the Los Angeles–Long Beach SMSA's. This, however, is not an unexpected trend, especially when viewed against the increasing equilibrium probabilities for the San Jose, Sacramento and San Diego SMSA's.

The most striking finding arising out of the equilibrium vectors in Table 7.7 is the overwhelming expected concentration of nonwhites in the Los Angeles and San Francisco regions. Of the projected nonwhite share for California, well over half are expected to settle in the Los Angeles–Long Beach SMSA and about a fifth should locate in the San Francisco–Oakland SMSA. This is in marked contrast to the allocation indicated by the white equilibrium vector. The latter exhibits a relatively more uniform probability distribution, though it too shows a significant concentration in the Los Angeles subregion.

Despite considerable differences between age-specific transition matrices, the equilibrium vectors of the six age groups analyzed in Tables 7.8, 7.9, and 7.10 are, on the whole, quite similar. The major difference appears in the California–Rest of the U.S. probability allocation. Thus, for example, whereas for the 20- to 24-year age group this division is 0.193–0.807, for the 65- to 69-year age group the corresponding split is 0.138–0.862. Among the five SMSA's, however, the vector does not vary substantially between age groups.

In the above paragraphs, we have borrowed concepts from Markov chain theory to identify and analyze migration differentials. Transition matrices were used to establish the movement propensities of each migrant cohort. Mean first passage times defined aspatial measures of interregional "migrant distance." Finally, equilibrium distributions pointed to the distributional tendencies of different classes of migrants.

The basic Markovian model is conceptually simple and rests on very strict assumptions concerning human behavior. Because of this, it is an analytic system which shows only limited promise as a tool for long-term forecasting of interregional flows. However, as a technique for analyzing differential behavior during an observed period, it appears to provide insights which are not readily obtainable by other means.

7.4. Analysis of Differentiated Streams

Having analyzed the statistical correlation between interregional migration and economic opportunity, and having then studied the differential characteristics of migrant streams, we conclude this chapter with a brief consideration of the joint effects of both dimensions on spatial mobility. Thus we report below the results of introducing class-specific flows into the model defined in (7.8).[19] It will be recalled this model assumed the form:

$$\ln M_{ij} = \beta_0 + \beta_1 \ln WS_i + \beta_2 \ln WS_j + \beta_3 \ln LF_i \\ + \beta_4 \ln LF_j + \beta_5 \ln D_{ij} + \epsilon_{ij}.$$

Several observations are suggested by the regression statistics presented in Tables 7.17 through 7.21. First, it appears that variations in interregional nonwhite flows are very weakly tied to spatial variations in economic opportunities, as reflected by per capita wages and salaries. Table 7.17 indicates that the factors motivating nonwhite migration are strikingly different from those inducing white movements and, moreover, are probably largely noneconomic in character. Whereas the Rogers model accounts for 80 percent of the total variance in the case of white flows, it only explains 27 percent of the total variation in nonwhite movements.

Ever since Dorothy Thomas's exhaustive findings on migration differentials, demographers have consistently asserted that young adults are the most mobile segment of the population. According to the statistics in Tables 7.18, 7.19, and 7.20, young adults also are the age group most responsive to spatial variations in economic opportunities. Their flows produce the highest R^2's in the Rogers model.

Finally, complementing the demographer's hypothesis that males are more mobile than females, we find strong indications in Table 7.21 that the economists's simple "economic opportunities" hypothesis is an inadequate framework with which to ac-

---

[19] Sex-specific flows were obtained from special tabulations of a 2 percent sample of reported changes of address in drivers' license registrations, supplied by the State Department of Motor Vehicles.

TABLE 7.17. REGRESSION STATISTICS FOR WHITE AND NONWHITE FLOWS

	A. White Flows			B. Nonwhite Flows	
Variable	Coefficient	Partial correlation coefficient	Variable	Coefficient	Partial correlation coefficient
Constant	−6.16275		Constant	−30.6021	
$\log LF_i$	0.77124***	0.67062	$\log LF_j$	2.63083***	0.29365
$\log LF_j$	0.67496***	0.62046	$\log LF_i$	1.83355***	0.20935
$\log D_{ij}$	−0.80346***	−0.65721	$\log D_{ij}$	−2.55513***	−0.26627
$\log WS_j$	0.28624	0.06989	$\log WS_j$	−1.65939	−0.04043
$\log WS_i$	−0.28436	−0.06944	$\log WS_i$	0.45730	0.01115
R^2	0.79983		R^2	0.26841	

*** Significant at the 0.1% level.

TABLE 7.18. COEFFICIENTS OF DETERMINATION FOR THE 17 AGE-SPECIFIC FLOW MATRICES

Age Group (years)	R^2
1. 0–4	0.79626
2. 5–9	0.78813
3. 10–14	0.79619
4. 15–19	0.80898
5. 20–24	0.81940
6. 25–29	0.81154
7. 30–34	0.81196
8. 35–39	0.80227
9. 40–44	0.78311
10. 45–49	0.51676
11. 50–54	0.78383
12. 55–59	0.52611
13. 60–64	0.53807
14. 65–69	0.45121
15. 70–74	0.37958
16. 75–79	0.29654
17. 80–84	0.37596

count for female migration. The Rogers model provides a satisfactory explanation of male movements but accounts for less than 45 percent of the total variation in female flows.

The statistics presented at the beginning and end of this chapter represent a modest attempt to assess the significance and relative weight of a set of economic variables and their differential impact on class-specific migrant streams. When considered together the results are promising. In almost every instance, variations in total flows have been accounted for by a small subset of variables. On the basis of these regression results we may justifiably conclude that comparative economic opportunity is a factor which significantly influences interregional movements in California. The results for differentiated streams are equally encouraging. The relatively well-established hypotheses of demographers concerning variations in behavior among classes of migrants appear again in the differential response of these migrant classes to economic opportunities. Thus we find that those

TABLE 7.19. REGRESSION STATISTICS FOR SELECTED AGE GROUP FLOWS

	A. 5–9 years		B. 20–24 years	
Variable	Coefficient	Partial correlation coefficient	Coefficient	Partial correlation coefficient
Constant	−6.99401		−10.4961	
$\log LF_j$	0.68531***	0.61956	0.80592***	0.69428
$\log LF_i$	0.74590***	0.65163	0.68350***	0.63322
$\log D_{ij}$	−0.80669***	−0.65213	−0.81398***	−0.66982
$\log WS_i$	−0.44112*	−0.10551	0.27630	0.06890
$\log WS_j$	0.27036	0.06489	−0.03608	−0.00902
R^2	0.78813		0.81940	

* Significant at the 5% level.
*** Significant at the 0.1% level.

TABLE 7.20. REGRESSION STATISTICS FOR SELECTED AGE GROUP FLOWS

	A. 40–44 years		B. 75–79 years		
Variable	Coefficient	Partial correlation coefficient	Variable	Coefficient	Partial correlation coefficient
Constant	−7.82173		Constant	−6.66146	
$\log LF_j$	0.68484***	0.61187	$\log LF_i$	1.60651***	0.34613
$\log LF_i$	0.75827***	0.65052	$\log LF_j$	1.28519***	0.28307
$\log D_{ij}$	−0.80202***	−0.64264	$\log D_{ij}$	−1.09556***	−0.22687
$\log WS_i$	−0.44236*	−0.10379	$\log WS_i$	−2.53454*	−0.12066
$\log WS_j$	0.26954	0.06345	$\log WS_j$	−0.50414	−0.02417
R^2	0.78311		R^2	0.29654	

* Significant at the 5% level.
*** Significant at the 0.1% level.

TABLE 7.21. REGRESSION STATISTICS FOR MALE AND FEMALE FLOWS

	A. Male Flows			B. Female Flows	
Variable	Coefficient	Partial correlation coefficient	Variable	Coefficient	Partial correlation coefficient
Constant	−11.0497		Constant	−13.0820	
$\log LF_i$	0.74863***	0.54917	$\log LF_j$	0.59556***	0.31637
$\log LF_j$	0.71096***	0.52301	$\log LF_i$	0.73050***	0.37861
$\log D_{ij}$	−0.74373***	−0.57681	$\log D_{ij}$	−0.69645***	−0.34358
$\log WS_i$	−0.14228	0.03140	$\log WS_j$	.73578	0.07711
$\log WS_j$	0.06331	0.01145	$\log WS_i$	−0.46286	−0.04860
R^2	0.77755		R^2	0.44484	

*** Significant at the 0.1% level.

classes which are more mobile also tend to be more sensitive to spatial variations in economic conditions.

7.5. References

[1] Beshers, James M. and Eleanor N. Nishuira, "A Theory of Internal Migration Differentials," *Social Forces*, 39 (1961), 214–218.

[2] Blumen, Isadore, Marvin Kogan and Philip J. McCarthy, *The Industrial Mobility of Labor as a Probability Process*, Vol. VI, Cornell Studies of Industrial and Labor Relations (Ithaca, New York: The New York State School of Industrial and Labor Relations, Cornell University, 1955).

[3] Bogue, Donald J., Henry S. Shryock, Jr. and Siegfried A. Hoermann, *Subregional Migration in the United States: 1935-40*, Vol. I (Oxford, Ohio: Scripps Foundation Studies in Population Distribution, Miami University, 1957).

[4] Bogue, Donald J. and Margaret Jarman Hagood, *Differential Migration in the Corn and Cotton Belts* (Oxford, Ohio: Scripps Foundation, 1953).

[5] Financial and Population Research Section, *California Migration: 1955-1960*, California Department of Finance, Sacramento, 1964.

[6] Kemeny, John G. and J. Laurie Snell, *Finite Markov Chains* (Princeton, N.J.: D. Van Nostrand Co., 1960), pp. 191–200.

[7] Lowry, Ira S., *Migration and Metropolitan Growth: Two Analytical Models* (San Francisco, Cal.: Chandler, 1966).

[8] Nelson, Phillip, "Migration, Real Income and Information," *Journal of Regional Science*, 1, no. 2 (Spring 1959), 43–62.

[9] Prais, S. J., "Measuring Social Mobility," *Journal of the Royal Statistical Society*, Series A (1955), pp. 56–66.

[10] Rogers, Andrei, "A Regression Analysis of Interregional Migration in California," *The Review of Economics and Statistics*, forthcoming.

[11] ———, "A Markovian Analysis of Migration Differentials," *Proceedings of the Social Statistics Section of the American Statistical Association*, 126th Annual Meeting (1966), 452–466.

[12] ———, *Projected Population Growth in California Regions: 1960-1980*, Center for Planning and Development Research,

University of California, Berkeley, California, December 1965.

[13] ———, *An Analysis of Interregional Migration in California*, Center for Planning and Development Research, University of California, Berkeley, California, December 1965.

[14] Tarver, James D. and William R. Gurley, "A Stochastic Analysis of Geographic Mobility and Population Projections of the Census Divisions in the United States," *Demography*, II (1965), 134–139.

[15] Thomas, Dorothy S., *Research Memorandum on Migration Differentials* (New York: Social Science Research Council, 1938), Bulletin 43.

[16] U.S. Bureau of the Census (PC(2)-2B), *U.S. Census of Population, 1960, Mobility for States and State Economic Areas*, U.S. Bureau of the Census, Department of Commerce, 1963.

8 CONCLUDING REMARKS

At the beginning of this essay, we observed that existing mathematical theories of demography were incomplete in that they ignored the effects of migration. Although populations undisturbed by migration may be adequate approximations of national population systems, they rarely are a workable abstraction of regional populations in multiregional settings. Space and time wield a joint influence on interregional population growth, and migration is the principal manifestation of their combined impact.

The subject of population and space is a broad one, combining the major concerns of demographers and ecologists. As one proceeds from studies of relatively "closed" national population systems to analyses of essentially "open" regions within multiregional systems, the importance of migration as a contributor to population change increases rapidly. Indeed, carrying the regional disaggregation even further, we find that at the *intra*regional or local community level, migration assumes primary importance and becomes the fundamental explanatory variable in studies of urban development patterns. Although at this level of disaggregation migration essentially manifests changes in residential locational behavior and reflects the influence of a fundamentally different set of variables, the shift from an *inter*regional to an *intra*regional problem focus may be accommodated within the same fundamental matrix model of population growth and distribution.

Consider, for example, an urban area that is divided into m zones. Introduce the following hypothesis: the residential population locates with respect to its place of employment. Assume, in short, that people, in striving to reduce the costs of their journey-to-work, tend to cluster in a regular manner around their places of employment. We may express this hypothesized relationship by the matrix equation

(8.1) $$\mathbf{w}^{(t)} = M\mathbf{e}^{(t)}$$

where $w_i^{(t)}$ = total population in the ith zone at time t;
$e_i^{(t)}$ = total employment in the ith zone at time t;
M = a matrix growth operator that transforms the employment vector, at time t, into the corresponding population vector, at time t.

If one assumes that employees live and work in the same zone, the matrix M may be interpreted as a diagonal matrix whose nonzero elements denote the population-per-employee ratios (i.e., the reciprocals of the zonal labor force participation rates) of the respective zones. More realistically, however, we may wish to assume that the residences of the employees working in each zone are distributed among all zones according to some observed inverse relationship with distance or travel time. Thus we may define m^*_{ij} as the proportion of employees, working in zone i, who live in zone j.[1] Expanding this proportion by the population-per-employee ratio of the jth zone, we may redefine the elements of the matrix M, as follows:

(8.2) $$m_{ij} = m^*_{ij}\alpha_j$$

where m^*_{ij} = proportion of employees who are employed in zone i and reside in zone j;
α_j = population-per-employee ratio of zone j.

Assume that employment growth and distribution may be represented by

(8.3) $$\mathbf{e}^{(t+1)} = S\mathbf{e}^{(t)}$$

where s_{ij} = the proportion of employees, working in zone i at time t, who are working in zone j at time $t + 1$;
s_{ii} = the sum of two proportions: (1) the proportion of employees, working in zone i at time t, who are working in zone i at time $t + 1$, and (2) the region's

---

[1] The author is grateful to a former student of his, Robert Garin, for this observation. See: Robert Garin, "A Matrix Formulation of the Lowry Model for Intrametropolitan Activity Allocation," *Journal of the American Institute of Planners*, XXXII:6 (November 1966), 361–364.

net "new" employees (i.e., "employee births" and employee-migrants into the urban areas less "employee-deaths" and employee-migrants out of the urban area) that are attributable to zone i, during the time interval $(t, t+1)$, as a proportion of total employees working in zone i at time t.

Then, by (8.1) and (8.3), we have

(8.4) $\qquad \mathbf{w}^{(t+1)} = M\mathbf{e}^{(t+1)} = MS\mathbf{e}^{(t)}.$

Consider now the population projection that is generated by an unchanging regime of employment growth and home-to-work structure. We have then

(8.5) $\qquad \mathbf{w}^{(t+n)} = MS^n\mathbf{e}^{(t)}$

and, therefore, may draw on the stability properties of nonnegative matrices, described in Chapter 5, to derive the stable rate of growth of the area's population and its stable spatial distribution.

Equation (8.1) relates the size and distribution of an area's population to the size and distribution of its employment. Earlier, in Chapter 2, we related the size and distribution of an interregional population to the size and distribution of that population at a previous time period as follows:

(8.6) $\qquad \mathbf{w}^{(t+1)} = G\mathbf{w}^{(t)}.$

By considering zones as regions we may use Equation (8.6) to describe the growth and distribution of an *intra*regional population and, in the process, establish a most useful relationship between the two alternative formulations. Combining (8.6) with (8.1), we have

(8.7) $\qquad \mathbf{w}^{(t+1)} = G\mathbf{w}^{(t)} = GM\mathbf{e}^{(t)}$

whence, by (8.4),

(8.8) $\qquad GM\mathbf{e}^{(t)} = MS\mathbf{e}^{(t)}$

and

(8.9) $\qquad G = MSM^{-1}$

or

(8.10) $\qquad S = M^{-1}GM.$

Concluding Remarks

Since it is generally more difficult to obtain empirical data for calibrating S than G, the relationship defined by (8.10) has considerable utility.

The above matrix formulation of *intra*regional population growth and distribution leads to a very simple and compact expression of an empirically verifiable relationship between the spatial patterns of population and employment in an urban area. It can be used to assess the spatial implications of changes in the size of the labor force and labor participation rates, and changes in accessibilities to employment centers. The model also relates employment growth to population growth and, more importantly, it readily accepts refinements in the hypothesized population-employment linkages. For example, the model may be extended to permit the distribution of employment and population, disaggregated into *basic* (export oriented) and *nonbasic* (service oriented) components, according to a more complicated locational rationale.[2]

In this monograph we have tried to identify space as a vital dimension that has been neglected by mathematical demographers. The early chapters of this essay have illustrated how this component might be included in the current matrix models of population systems. Subsequent chapters focused on some of the more interesting problems and questions that such an approach generates. Finally, we have briefly outlined how the matrix formulation can be extended to describe intraregional, as well as interregional, population systems. In sum, our efforts represent an attempt to bring population mathematics to bear on spatial questions. It is our hope that the results might stimulate others to devote more attention to this problem. Possibly our findings may serve as a point of departure for such efforts.

[2] *Ibid.*

INDEX

Age-specific flow matrices, 17, 21
Age-specific rates:
  birth rates, 10
  migration proportions, 11–13, 26
  net migration rates, 11
  survivorship rates, 10
Algebra, matrix, 2. *See also* Matrices

Beshers, James M., 82
Blumen, Isadore, 2 n., 85 n.
Bogue, Donald J., 82, 93 n.
Bram, Joseph, 42 n.

California, demographic data:
  age composition, 28
  age-specific birth rates, 14, 20
  age-specific flow matrix, 23
  age-specific migration proportions, 14, 23, 26, 96–99
  age-specific survivorship rates, 14, 20
  components of change, 8, 36
  distributional goals and system intervention, 61–64
  distribution of net migration, 21
  distribution of population, 24, 27
  equilibrium distributions, 101–104
  forecasts, 22–29
  growth operator, 14
  intrinsic rate of growth, 49–51
  mean first passage times, 96–101
  migration differentials, 92–104
  migration stream analysis, 76–82, 104–110
  migration transition matrices, 9, 19–20, 23, 24–28, 93–96
  stable interregional age structure, 51
  stable interregional population distribution, 49–50
  survivorship matrix, 19, 20, 22–24
California Department of Finance, 92 n.
Characteristic roots and characteristic vectors, 32, 48–49
Cohort-survival models, 1
  interregional, 11–13
  simplified interregional, 16–18
  single-region, 10–11
  stable interregional age structure, 50–51
Collar, A. R., 32 n.
Collinearity transformation, 31
Components of change models, 1
  interregional, 7–10
  single-region, 6–7
  stable interregional population distribution, 49

Debreu, G., 4 n.
Declining population system, 64, 66
Determinental equation, 32
Distances, interregional, 25, 26
Distributional goals, 53
Duncan, W. J., 32 n.

Economic opportunity and migration, 4–5, 24–25, 73–80

Estimation, 3
  by temporal decomposition, 31–35
  on the basis of distributional data, 35–43
Estimators, 37
  minimum absolute deviations, 39–40
  restricted least-squares, 42–43
  unrestricted least-squares, 38–39
Equilibrium distributions, 90
Expanding population system, 70

Fisher, W. D., 37 n.
Flow matrices. *See* Age-specific flow matrices
Forecasting, 16–30
Frazer, R. A., 32 n.
Frobenius, Georg F., 48

Garin, Robert, 113 n.
Goal distribution, 54
Growth operator. *See* Operator
Gurley, William R., 3 n., 85 n.

Hagood, Margaret Jarman, 82
Hamilton, C. H., 3 n.
Herstein, I. N., 4 n.
Hoermann, Siegfried A., 82 n., 93 n.

Interregional distances, 26
Interregional transition matrix, 12
Intervention, 4
  declining population, full control, 66–67
  declining population, partial control, 67–68, 69
  expanding population, full control, 70–71
  in California regions, 61–64
  stationary population, full control, 55–58
  stationary population, partial control, 58–61

Intraregional population growth and distribution, 118
Isard, Walter, 2

Journey-to-work, 112
Judge, G. G., 37 n.

Karlin, Samuel, 48 n.
Kemeny, John G., 53 n., 56, 89
Kemeny-Snell Theorem, 56
Keyfitz, Nathan, 2 n., 10 n.
Kogan, Marvin, 2 n., 85 n.

Labor force eligibles, 25–26, 78
Labor force participation rate, 113, 115
Linear programming, 39–40
Linear regression, 25–26, 38
Little, Arthur D., Inc., 25 n.
Lopez, Alvaro, 2 n., 10 n.
Lowry, Ira S., 74 n.
Lowry model, 74
  modified, 76–78
Lowry-Rogers model, 78

McCarthy, Philip J., 2 n., 85 n.
McGinnis, Robert, 85 n.
Madansky, A., 37 n.
Markov chains:
  applications, 85
  ergodic, 92
  mean first passage times, 87–90
  migration differential analysis, 86
  transition matrices, 87, 91
Matrices, 2–3, 5
  fertility-survivorship, 18
  net migration, 18
  nonnegative, 4, 47–49
  population, 18
  reducible, 48 n.
Mean first passage times, 87–90
Migrant distance, 90
Migration, 4–5
  and economic opportunities, 74–80
  differential analysis, 82–92

Index

intraregional, 112
stream analysis, 73–82
transition matrices, 9, 17, 19, 24, 34. See also Transition matrices
Miller, George A., 37 n.
Miller, Robert, 3 n.
Models. See Cohort-survival models; Components of change models
Murphy, E. M., 50 n.

National Planning Association, 26 n.
Nelson, Phillip, 82 n.
Nishiura, Eleanor N., 82
Nonnegative matrices, theory of, 4, 47–49

Operator:
estimation of. See Estimation
growth, 7, 9, 11, 13
migration, 10, 12
survivorship, 11

Perron, Oskar, 47
Pilger, John E., 85 n.
Prais, S. J., 85 n.

Quadratic programming, 42

Regression, multiple linear, 26, 38
analysis of migration proportions, 26
analysis of migration streams, 74–76

Residential location, 112
Rey, Guido, 37 n.
Rogers, Andrei, 3 n., 16 n., 25 n., 86 n., 93 n.
Rogers model, 80, 104, 106

Saaty, Thomas L., 42 n.
Shryock, Henry S., Jr., 82 n., 93 n.
Siegel, J. S., 3 n.
Simplex algorithm, 42
Snell, J. Laurie, 53 n., 56, 89
Solow, R. M., 4 n.
Stable distribution, 47, 49
Stable rate of growth, 47
Stability, 3–4, 46–51
Stationary population system, 54
Survivorship matrix, 11, 19, 20, 22

Takayama, T., 37 n.
Tarver, James D., 3 n., 85 n.
Telser, Lester G., 39
Theil, Henry, 37 n.
Thomas, Dorothy S., 82, 104
Transition matrices, 12, 87, 91–92, 93. See also Migration transition matrices

U. S. Bureau of the Census, 19 n., 74 n., 93 n.

Wages and salaries, per capita, 25, 26, 78
Wagner, Harvey M., 37 n.
Wolfe, Phillip, 42
Woodbury, Max A., 4 n.

Soc
HB
885
R57